HEALTHCARE DESIGN AND OTHER OXYMORONS

HEALTHCARE DESIGN AND OTHER OXYMORONS

BY

NICK DEVENNEY

BOOK DESIGN BY

STEPHANIE WADE

www.bookstandpublishing.com

Published by
Bookstand Publishing
Morgan Hill, CA 95037
3253_2

ISBN 978-1-58909-864-0

Printed in the United States of America

DEDICATION

 This book is dedicated to my wife Joany without whose help and coaching this book would never have been completed; instead lying half finished in the pile with my other good intentions. She is my guide and anchor, providing both direction and stability.

 Also, a special thank you to Stephanie Wade, my unflappable right hand woman for eleven years, who guides me through the mysteries of computer generated document design and construction. The book cover design is another example of Stephanie's talent.

ACKNOWLEDGEMENTS

Offered so you know who is to blame for what I am.

Alfred R. Shands, Jr., MD, A pioneer in orthopedic surgery, who agreed to perform what at the time, early 1940s, was a very risky pediatric spinal fusion. Dr. Shands has passed away, so this posthumous thanks is for literally saving my life.

My parents who loved me so much they sold all their possessions and left their family and friends to take me from Wilmington, Delaware to Phoenix in 1948, based on a misdiagnosis that indicated I had rheumatic fever and needed to move to a dry climate.

My semi nuclear family consisting of Barbi, my first wife, and our kids Barry and Lauri Devenney, and Joany, now my wife, and our kids Ron and Steve Bennett. I have put this team through much unpleasantness and through it all I know I still have their support that I don't deserve. After reading this book you will agree that they have put up with a major nutcase. Their continued love is a mystery to me.

Mr. R.E. McCullar, Men's Dean, Phoenix Union High School, who was my advisor during the wild ride of my high school years at old P.U. Because my dysfunctional health kept me out of the public school system until my entrance at P.U. as a freshman, Mr. McCullar recognized I might need help adapting to groups of more than ten. I would not have made it without his many "readmits" from my several expulsions.

Frank Lloyd Wright, who in the mid '50s taught me most of what I know about architectural design, but I didn't realize it until recently.

.

Miles Stahm, my partner for eighteen years through thick and thin. We learned a great deal from each other, including that we will be friends forever.

 **Carol Mook,** who was originally a client, then joined our firm in 1983 as manager of a property management company I owned. Her arrival coincided with the discovery that my CFO, a personal friend for many years, had embezzled several hundred thousand dollars pushing us close to bankruptcy. An angel called Carol stepped in and managed a complete work-out, paying all creditors 100% - a miracle. Carol stayed for another twenty-five years, as our CFO, managing our finances and me thorough a growth from five people to over sixty, becoming a major architectural practice. Carol ranks with Dr. Shands as my life saver, and a dear friend.

Several local architects mentioned in the book who greatly helped me mature through my apprenticeship in a very difficult profession, providing me the opportunity to become a registered architect in 1964. My dream.

This may seem like a short list. But it is a list of people that gave, and continue to give, powerful support for me. If there is any good in this book, you now know where it came from.

Introduction, Prologue, Forward, Preamble, Whatever.

If you have ever experienced prolonged contact with Architects, you know they are a subspecies that sees the world through kaleidoscopic glasses – nothing focused, ever-changing, unpredictable, and beautiful. This book is a peek through a pair of those glasses – mine. We will ricochet from opinions to experiences to poems to philosophies, arranged in no particular order, straight from my pinball mind.

I have always known I wanted to be an architect, virtually springing from the womb "T" square in hand. Maybe that's why Mother never liked me. Most architects will tell you they have always known they wanted to be an architect. One does not dabble in various jobs and eventually decide to try architecture next. Architecture is an easily identifiable job, like a fireman or doctor, which children can understand and adopt at an early age. Professions like insurance agent, union boss, or florist don't seem to light the fire of a five year old. But an architect – wow!

Unfortunately architects do not have hero status like firemen or doctors. Architects are much maligned, I think by bad rumors started by evil contractors. Stuff like "Architects can't keep a budget, can't meet a schedule, and can't stop leaks, cracks or squeaks." All this is very true. We have good reasons but exploring them has already been done in stunning boredom in many other books. Not this one.

Some of my friends (I think) have read parts of this book as it was being written and have questioned why I would mix so many topics – healthcare, sustainability, religion, growing up, politics, ethics, etc. – into a book about the practice of architectural design. The answer is that every one of these topics influences architecture and, to a great extent, architecture influences them.

There cannot be a serious discussion about the design of a church, or a town, or a hospital without understanding the relationships that civility, politics, religion etc. have on design goals.

So skip around, read the parts you like and avoid parts that you don't agree with. Maybe later you will go back to the skipped parts. I hope

CONTENTS

THE START OF
A LONG ROAD TO NOWHERE SPECIFIC

WITH INTERESTING STOPS
ALONG THE WAY ....

START
HERE

IF YOU SEEK TRUTH
AND ENLIGHTENMENT
STOP NOW!
PLEASURE SEEKERS
PLEASE CONTINUE.

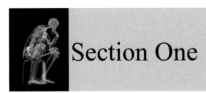 Section One

The book title describes my life as **<u>A saga without end – yet</u>** People have questioned why I chose "saga" to describe my life. **Saga**, per Webster; *"**A long story of adventure and heroic deeds.**"* I figured one and a half out of three was good enough. My story is long, seventy five years so far, weak on adventure, and devoid of heroism. Also note the title says "observations", not instructions. You will find more questions than answers in here, which I guess is normal life.

Having sucked you in with my trick title I wish I could tell you this book will enlighten you about architecture, revealing the rivalry's of great architects, offering deep debate about the meaning of design, etc. It won't. My architectural interest is focused on designing buildings to promote healing – basically hospitals. A very challenging specialty. Winston Churchill supposedly said "first we shape our buildings, thereafter they shape us;" or something like that.

I like to think forming hospitals creates a structural tool that can help its occupants in their battle to overcome illness or injury. As we will see, there is a real opportunity for buildings to be a <u>part of</u> the healing process, not just a box that contains it. I think that is pretty exciting. But as you will discover it is only one topic covered herein and sporadically at that.

1

I am not a famous architect, but I have known some. So this book is not about the life of a famous architect, but just about me. Unlike books by famous architects this one does not preach, or rationalize a particular doctrine of architectural design. In fact there is not so much about architecture, probably just more about life ideas and my personal opinions.

You probably have discovered there are no chapters in this book. It is not a mistake. If you purchased this book thinking you would get a focused discussion about a particular subject, get your money back now.

"Chapters" indicate an orderly progression or continuation of a theme. This book, having no theme or order, is instead loosely separated into "sections" to provide easy stopping points for food or potty breaks, or giving up entirely. Hey, just because you bought the whole book doesn't mean you need to read the whole thing.

Being afflicted with Attention Deficit Disorder provides me with many blessings not afforded normal people, one of which is an inability to boringly focus for long periods of time on a single subject.

This book is about my ideas, opinions and experiences, presented in a more or less stream of consciousness, or semi consciousness. Think of it as the longest blog you will ever read. If I was somebody, this would be a book worth reading. Instead, this is a book worth writing, a therapeutic monologue that allows me to expound without interruption or dissent. It doesn't get any better than that! And the best part is I can't type, which masks my poor spelling. Joany, my wife/partner, types <u>and</u> provides spelling simultaneously. All I need to do is scribble.

Also, being an architect, I am professionally exempt from plebian concerns like proper spelling. My profession has arrogantly self proclaimed itself to be the "pattern givers to society". God help you. Less is more, more or less, I guess.

Architects are much maligned because we can't spell. Through the years my mother, teachers, secretaries, lawyers, clients, etc. have all assumed I am mentally challenged in some fashion. I believe architects have difficulty spelling because we see the possible option for arrangement of the parts of a whole as irrelevant so long as the outcome achieves the overall design goal, like arranging letters to form words. In support of my opinion, I submit the following:

> I cdnuolt blveiee taht I cluod aulacity uesdnatnrd waht I was rdanieg. The phaonmneal pweor of the humuan mnid aoccdrnig to a rscheerch at Cmabrigde Uinervtisy, it deosn't mttaer inwaht oredr the ltteers in a wrod are, the olny ipmoatnt tihng is taht the frist and lsat ltteer be in the rghit pclae. The rset can be a taotl mses and you can sitll raed it woutnit a porbelm. Tihs is bcuseae the huamn mnid deos not raed ervey lteter by istlef, but the word as a wlohe. Amzanig huh? Yaeh and you awlyas thought sipeling was ipmorantt!

3

Growing up. A topic worth exploring so you will "know where I'm coming from" (or came from), and "where I'm at" (not always sure). Do you "see what I'm say'n?"

Well let's start at my beginning – Mom and Dad, the very seeds of my existence. These folks were truly what is now referred to as old school, probably because they actually grew up in that era of loyalty, commitment, duty, personal accountability, responsibility, patriotism and respect for authority. Traits that have increasingly been modified to allow living up to easier standards, spurred to new heights in the '60s with the mantra that undercut everything – "question authority" – with its implied promise that all rules could be modified in one's mind, allowing the comfort of rationalization. Notice the phrase says "question", not "defy".

Questioning authority transitioned from meaning "reasoned debate" to "modify governing systems", urging each individual to make their own modifications and live their lives accordingly. The revelation of questioning authority came late in my maturation, but nonetheless allowed me a measure of guilt free (mostly) defiance, such as jaywalking and avoiding the recommended daily doses of leafy green vegetables.

Mom, Charlotte Hamilton, met Dad, Edman Devenney, in the first grade in Wilmington, Delaware and never parted until, as the vow says, death did them part. Both were children of immigrants (legal) from Ireland and Scotland. Growing up at the turn of the century – (the last one) – they lived in hard times that made those aforementioned values a necessity for survival. Not just for individuals, but for society in general. Eventually

4

their first grade crush evolved into a marriage. Unfortunately, Mom was a Protestant and Dad a Catholic which made no difference to them, or to the Hamilton family, but to the Papist Devenney clan it was intolerable.

Somehow the marriage took place, saving me from being a technical bastard, but there persist some who still refer to me as "that bastard Devenney." So on October 18, 1934 the blessed event occurred. I was baptized in the Catholic Church. The first step in my winding pathway seeking truth and enlightenment. I have not yet reached the end.

As luck would have it Mom's plumbing was not well constructed for baby making so, after my difficult entry act, science rescinded her fertility capacities insuring that I would be an only child. A situation the State of Delaware adoption system would reverse, but more about my sister Peggy later.

I was a "difficult baby." Right away I developed an amazing ability to acquire every virus, bacteria and allergen within five miles. This required keeping me home from school for huge chunks of time, possibly for the safety of the neighborhood as much as concern for me. I was toxic. Accordingly Mom had little time to pursue a career other than homemaker and pediatric nurse – two of our most valued professions.

One of my favorite hobbies while just lying around being sick was to dream up inventions or improvements like bathtubs with the drain at the opposite end of the faucets, making rinsing the tub easier. Or cars designed with the driver on the curb side to allow exit without stepping into traffic and providing better curb vision when parking. I stopped suggesting my ideas to my parents because their constant query was "if you're so smart why aren't you rich?" Having never developed a snappy retort I became a shy introvert, stifling my genius.

Dad had many talents, - theatre manager, drummer, advertisement, graphic artist, and machinist. Additionally, he was not opposed to performing tasks for which he had no talent, especially home improvement projects. This explained his many trips to the Emergency Department for electric shock, falls, animal bites, fractures, adverse inhalations, removal of foreign bodies and temporary blindness. Being untrained and accident prone is a bad mix. His escapades became family legends, ranging from three cracked ribs from walking into a parking meter while ogling a pretty girl, to discovering (repeatedly) that using ungrounded power tools while barefoot in wet grass can have shocking consequences.

Mom also had her moments. She was excellent in all things except one – cooking. It wasn't until I moved out and got married that I discovered how liver and onions are supposed to taste. Mom's version was to toss slabs of liver into a pan, set on low heat, and cook until she deemed it to be "well done". The result was a gourmet treat few outside the family have experienced - a piece of liver dried to a supple leathery consistency, impossible to cut, to be eaten as a finger food. I would try to put mine under the table for Prince, our dog, who worried it for hours as a chew toy.

Around the age of six or seven, Mom noticed that my right side was slowly going paralyzed. No, it was not from our liver diet. Fortunately because of her persistence, the doctors of the early '40s stopped telling her it was "just a growing phase" and correctly diagnosed that my spine was defective, slowly trying to sever the spinal cord.

Unfortunately in those days nobody knew how to fix it. Fortunately, a relatively new hospital had opened up about ten miles from our house – The Alfred I. DuPont De Nemours Institute. It specialized in treating pediatric surgical cases other hospitals considered too risky. The hospital sits in the middle of the A.I. DuPont estate, a gorgeous setting, and was, (and still is I think) totally underwritten by the DuPont family.

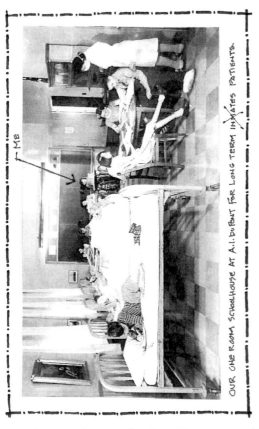

OUR ONE ROOM SCHOOLHOUSE AT A.I. DuPONT FOR LONG TERM INMATES PATIENTS.

ME

Doubly fortunate for me was that a genius in pediatric spines took a keen interest in how my sort of condition could be fixed – Alfred R. Shands, Jr., M.D. Medical Director Emeritus.

I was a guest of Mr. DuPont during most of WWII, (I wasn't draft age anyway), while Dr. Shands evaluated, experimented, and then performed the miracle that saved me from death or paralysis.

I don't recall how long I was incarcerated, but when Mom and Dad took me there they promised me a horse if I would be a good boy. My stay was long enough to allow Dad to buy a horse, build a barn by himself, (without serious injury), adopt a little girl, and have the horse die, buy another horse (healthier), return the first little girl and adopt a new one (nicer) – my sister, Peggy.

So homecoming had surprises – a new horse, a new barn and a new sister. And the added surprise to be learned at my discharge, (in a full body brace), that I was not to ride horses, among other activities.

We sold the horse, kept the sister, and converted the barn to a workshop. Devenneys are very flexible.

After "graduation" from A.I. DuPont I began having strange swelling episodes, made difficult because the maker of my leather and steel body brace did not anticipate me turning into a blimp. Our doctors didn't seem to know what I had, but nonetheless prescribed an en mass shift of the Devenney Clan to "a hot dry climate". The consensus was that Arizona would fit the bill.

Without any hesitation my parents decided to leave everything and everyone they knew and loved to get me to Arizona. They had barely a high school education evidenced by their belief, after consulting maps, that we all would need passports so we could travel across a foreign country – New Mexico – to get to Arizona. I point this out not to belittle, or for laughs, but to emphasize how terrifying it must have been for them. Arizona was as unknown to them as Mongolia, but when the doctor said their "Nicky" needed to move to Arizona, they unquestioningly acted immediately. You gotta love people like that – especially if you're their son.

We arrived by train in Phoenix in July, 1948. Welcome to Hades! We picked the right spot for hot and dry. And no air-conditioning. And voila! – I healed within days. Never have found out what I had.

I was13, eighth grade age, but had to take the State of Arizona education placement test. The results indicated I could start as a junior in high school. I was elated. My folks were not. They insisted I begin as a high school freshman, which I did on a campus of 5,000 students, at Phoenix Union High School, old P.U. About 15 kids in one place was as big a group as I had encountered until then. Apparently my social skills were unformed, and a full four years at P.U. proved invaluable in molding me into the socially smooth person I am today. Another smart decision by Mom and Dad.

After a childhood of miscellaneous diseases, injuries and surgeries, my time at old P.U. was a continuous celebration and exploration of life as a healthy person, able to do normal things. And also some abnormal things. Unleashed on the world, I became a driven joiner – Drama club, Oratorio Society, Debate Club, etc. plus non-school activities like the Phoenix Light Opera Company.

I loved the Opera Company. Although short on talent I was long on chutzpah, gaining minor parts in the *Mikado, Rigelleto, Die Fledermaus* as well as Broadway shows such as *Oklahoma, Student Prince, Vagabond King and Carousel.* These shows often required evening rehearsals lasting past midnight. Such extra curricular activities plus the P.U. demands was my way of pushing Mother Nature to make up for lost time. When I entered P.U. I was six feet tall, 170 pounds. Upon exit four years later I was six feet tall, 126 pounds. Yes, it is possible to burn your candle at both ends, but the results are not always pleasing.

I was also interested in science. As the chemistry teacher's pet, I had access to the chemical storage room so that I could assist in setting out class experiments. Among the exotic chemicals available was a large block of sodium, a soft metal. Sodium has a spectacular reaction to air and water and therefore it is stored under kerosene. I undertook a self-designed, extra curricular experiment involving wrapping a sizable chunk of sodium in a kerosene soaked paper towel and stuffing it down a toilet bowl. To this day the boy's restroom bears testimony to the explosive power of nature, fortunately not traced to moi. Although I have heard of copy cat versions over the years, most recently in Jodi Picoult's book *Handle with Care*, for the record, I must state my experiment in 1952 predates all other claims for similar experiments.

Another science experiment, this time in physics, required the assistance of several friends and its successful conclusion earned me a twenty dollar prize (bet), a princely sum in 1952. I was able to prove a Crosley, "sports car" (a mid 50s minicar) could be supported by the grand piano in the auditorium. Unfortunately, the owner of the car, a teacher, and the owner of the piano, P.U., were not impressed. Great breakthroughs in science are often initially misunderstood. Ask Mr. Galileo.

In addition to constantly expanding my horizons in the sciences and arts my retarded socialization skills needed constant attention. Several fellow students – older, having returned to P.U. after serving in the Korean "conflict" – had skills far beyond most high school students.

With Phoenix being located only 181 miles from Nogales, Mexico, we had easy access to the cultures and customs of border town nightlife. These international forays also provided income opportunities. We bought strong spirits at very low cost in Mexico for resale at very high profits to the guests of the Westward Ho Hotel, one of Phoenix's plushiest spots in the '50s.

I should make clear that the statute of limitations has expired on all of the above petty crimes and misdemeanors.

# Section Two

Towards the end of high school (the most fun packed four years of my life!) I decided to try to join Frank Lloyd Wright's Architectural Fellowship at Taliesin. I had known since birth that I wanted to be an architect and, what luck, one of the world's greatest architects resided only fifteen miles from my high school, Phoenix Union, old P.U. Don't laugh, lots of great people other than me graduated from P.U.

As graduation loomed ending my four year combination socialization, education (some), and non-stop party, I decided to visit Mr. Wright to see if I could become an apprentice. So towards the end of my senior year I ditched school and drove to Taliesin West, north of Scottsdale, over fifteen miles of very bad dirt road. Now a major freeway zooms past Taliesin. Progress.

I was fortunate that the first person I encountered at Taliesin was Mr. Wright, who was alone in his studio, door open, opening mail. We had a long "conversation", meaning I listened to Mr. Wright expound on a variety of topics for over two hours. What a phenomenal experience! A green dumb kid not yet out of high school getting a one on one with Frank Lloyd Wright <u>and</u> getting accepted to apprenticeship. I told him I would not be able to start for two months because my high school graduation wasn't until June. His reply – "Come right now, you will learn what you need here". At the time I didn't know of Mr. Wright's disdain for schools of

"Regard it as just as desirable to build a chicken house as to build a cathedral. The size of the project means little in art, beyond the money matter. It is the quality of character that really counts. Character may be large in the little, or little in the large." Frank Lloyd Wright, 1931, Chicago Art Institute Lecture.

architecture. I went directly home and started packing, intending to move to Taliesin West and join the Fellowship's spring migration to Taliesin East in Spring Green, Wisconsin, and dedicating myself to being Mr. Wright's apprentice.

Until recently being an apprentice was the ancient way to become an architect – learning by doing under a mentor. In Arizona in the '50s the State Registration Board rules provided that after eight years of acceptable apprenticeship you could sit for the state examination for licensure as an architect. That system is under constant pressure from universities to include a degree from an accredited school of architecture as part of the application requirements for examination. The role of licensure is to protect the public health, safety and welfare, issues given very little emphases in school but are part of everyday work as an apprentice in a functioning architectural practice. Draw your own value conclusions.

Fortunately my parents exerted parental control, informing me they had no idea who this Frank Lloyd Wright was, or what Taliesin was, but they did know I wasn't going anywhere until I graduated from P.U. Another one of the many times Mom and Dad saved my irrational ass. So I missed the Taliesin migration, instead going to Spring Green on the first Greyhound the morning after graduation.

So started an amazing two years, picking strawberries, hauling rocks, arranging flowers, watching architects, watching architecture, kitchen duty, Sunday dinners, breakfast talks, famous visitors, drafting, drafting,

drafting, music, watching Mr. Wright, avoiding Mrs. Wright, becoming aware. In retrospect, Taliesin was my most valuable architectural learning experience, learning that architecture is more than just buildings, understanding the powerful shape of space, the volatile volume contained within and around the feeble constructions we call architecture.

I noticed that most of the apprentices had been at Taliesin for many years, and apparently had little intention to leave. A lifetime hitch. My holy grail was to become an architect as soon as possible, establish my own office, and recruit my own clients. This goal

MR. WRIGHT ON PATROL AT TALIESIN, APPARENTLY UNAWARE THAT ALL OF HIS CREATIVITY WAS CHANNELD THRU MRS. WRIGHT AND HER LOONEY FRIEND.— A PERSONAL OPINION. MINE.

required taking a state examination to become a duly licensed registered architect, which I thought could be expedited with some formalized education. I suspected Taliesin was not that pathway, so I left. Fortunately, for two reasons.

First, I did get on a legitimate track to registration. Unbeknownst to me, the Arizona State Registration Board at that time held a strong dislike for Mr. Wright because he refused to get registered in Arizona. Consequently, any apprenticeship time I served under one of the world's great architects was unacceptable to the Arizona Board, and therefore useless towards my getting registered.

Secondly I left before I understood the deeper darker culture of Taliesin, detailed in the book *The Fellowship,* by Roger Friedland and Harold Zellman. Mrs. Wright believed all of Mr. Wright's creativity was due to her teaching him the philosophies of Gurdjieff (go to Wikipedia) a view not widely held since Mr. Wright was a world success long before Mrs. Wright, (Olgivana) arrived at Taliesin. My opinion on the subject is summarized on page 512 of *The Fellowship,* quote: "*When apprentice Nick Devenney heard Olgivana make the same claim during one of her spiritual groups, he couldn't hide the doubt on his face. 'I see we have somebody here who does not agree,' the ever-vigilant Olgivanna announced to the others. For Devenney, that was his first and last exposure to Olgivanna's teachings. He had come to study Mr. Wright's architecture, he said, not Mrs. Wright's "bullshit"*..

Yes, I was a diplomat, even at an early age. The book details a Taliesin that was not evident to me. If it had been, my Taliesin tenure would have been even shorter.

I determined early that a long term relationship with Mrs. Wright would be to our mutual detriment. That, coupled with a growing realization that even a renowned genius can sometimes provide conflicting direction to a budding young genius (that would be me), by simultaneously building two homes side by side in the Arizona desert. One, the Boomer residence, of desert stone similar to Taliesin West and the other, the Adleman residence, a concrete block system known as Usonian, developed for a different climate.

I was one of the lucky apprentices who got to stay in Phoenix over the 110 degree summer to construct them. All the unlucky apprentices had to go to Wisconsin for the summer.

The juxtaposition of dissimilar design concepts totally clashed with Mr. Wright's dictum of a building reflecting and respecting its site. As I worked constructing them I wondered which one was correct. The only commonality was a sewer leach field that served both of them, requiring endless hours laying on a jackhammer in Arizona in July. Lessons in architecture are not always enjoyable.

The Taliesin mask had slipped enough that I felt it was time to move on and experience a different educational process, so I entered what was eventually to become a top College of Architecture at Arizona State University.

Emphasis on "eventually". In the mid 1950s (yes, in the 20th century) it consisted of a faculty of two, Mr. Jim Elmore and Mr. Mel Ensign, occupying half of a war surplus "Quonset hut". For those under fifty, look it up.

Elmore and Ensign struggled mightily to pull together a meaningful, motivational, architectural curriculum. However, I found other interesting courses. I found that business, chemistry, English (yes smarty, I did take English), girls, physics, fine art (which curiously does not include architecture), history, drinking, archaeology, etc., etc. formed a perfect curriculum for a person with attention deficit disorder and poor work ethics.

Academia for me was secondary to the real work I was fortunate to get apprenticing with several Phoenix Architects: Fred Weaver, Stan Stein, Chuck Hickman, Francis Bricker, Earl Horlbeck, Al Beadle, Gene Buchli and Murray Harris. These guys, most now gone, were a vanishing, perhaps now vanished, breed that made the apprenticeship system work – they spent much of their time mentoring the young, providing values that "formal education" will never achieve. And the University took my money while my mentors paid me!

I have been told one of the values of a college education is to obtain a "world view." I have yet to meet a professor whose world view I would like to learn; for example, my physics professor who would swoon over Saul Alinski's latest radical thoughts, or my English professor who was on a daily vendetta against the Government spending money on this "space stuff" – in 1956 – a true visionary! Somehow I did not value the world view of a group of people whose idea of success is

19

obtaining tenure, and who seemed to have an ill concealed distrust and resentment towards the off-campus working world.

Interruption. I am writing now in John Wayne Airport in Orange County, California watching a woman, almost seven feet tall, approximately one hundred ten pounds, dressed in a black lycra body suit and seven inch spiked heels, wearing a long white bridal veil featuring large white Mickey Mouse ears. Isn't nature's diversity awe inspiring? Then again, I am in California.

It has been said that those who can't, teach. I think this is an unfair statement. Architecture professors are very talented designers. The problem is they primarily design for themselves, not for a client. You will often hear architects refer to their designs as "my buildings." Successful practicing architects know they really are not "their" buildings, but instead belong to their clients. Architects who don't grasp this subtle distinction will paint a building purple even though their client, who owns the building, hates purple. These folks belong in a university job where their narcissistic tendencies can be freely enjoyed, designing in a vacuum for themselves, unfettered by a pesky owner.

As a young idealist I worked my butt off trying to make the design of a hotel I was working on as good as it could be. My bubble was burst by the owner, Ernie Uhllman, who very succinctly described to me his view of the building's purpose vs. what I thought was the purpose of a building and the duty of an architect, as conveyed to me by my mentor of the moment, Frank L. Wright.

Ernie provided me an architectural epiphany – viewing buildings as <u>investments</u> rather than as <u>objects</u>. Stocks, bonds, commodities, futures, options – and buildings.

"For you, it is a building. For me it is a tool to make money." Ernie Uhllman, 1955.

"Every building has a duty to enhance and promote the collective beauty of its community, and its site," Frank L. Wright, 1955.

Wright saw buildings as an opportunity and a duty for architects to promote "the collective beauty".

Uhllman saw buildings as a business cost – only one of many line items of a project's feasibility analysis.

Who is right – Wright or Uhllman? They both are, which makes architecture so challenging. We must accept that there is no wrong or right to these differing definitions of "building" – both are valid expectations. Good aesthetics are sometimes embraced purely for pride of ownership reasons. However, more often aesthetics are employed for competitive reasons – being the best looking bank – <u>as a business/investment decision, not an architectural decision</u>.

Unfortunately for architects, there are far more "Ernies" than "Franks", and since we prefer Franks' view, we constantly try to turn Ernies into Franks. To have any chance of success in performing that transformation we need to study and understand the Ernie mind, buy business econ books instead of architectural books.

Read *"Forbes"* & *"Entrepreneur"* magazines instead of *Architectural Record.*

Typically architects consider creativity as finding creative solutions for aesthetic, functional and technical issues. We seldom include creative solutions for economic and investment issues that meet the owner's strategic and business plan goals.

LOU RUVO CENTER FOR BRAIN HEALTH
LAS VEGAS, NEVADA

I DID NOT MAKE THIS UP! GO TO WIKIPEDIA FILE: LOU RUVO CENTER - CLOSEUP - 2010-03-05. JPG FOR THE ORIGINAL PHOTO.

RESEARCH FUNDS ARE PRECIOUS — SPEND THEM WISELY.....

Complete business plans conclude with an "exit strategy," which in building ownership means how long will our client own the building, and how will it be disposed, i.e. sold, change of use, leased, renovated, demolished, expanded. How often do we present flexible conversion or expandability as a creative business option – without being asked?

Few building types are controlled by Franks. Those that are include single family residential, certain public buildings, churches and – sometimes – hospitals, more or less. However, even hospital clients swiftly transform from a Frank to an Ernie when contemplating a freestanding outpatient center, or a medical office building.

That transformation places special expectations on our services. Unlike a hospital building, the outpatient or medical office building project is considered primarily as a tool to make money, directly or indirectly. Directly from operational profit, or indirectly by attracting physician practices to the campus. These are unique buildings having very special needs and goals – as investments.

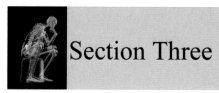

Section Three

What is an architect? Technically it is one who is licensed to practice architecture by the state, or states, in which they perform services. There are many very talented and knowledgeable persons that can perform high quality architectural services, but unless they are licensed to do so they are not legally an architect.

Many architects put A.I.A. after their name, meaning they belong to the major professional association for architects, the American Institute of Architects. The correct appellation is RA, registered architect, but it is rarely used. Why? I don't know. Doctors do not put AMA (American Medical Association) after their name to designate that they are a doctor – they put M.D., Medical Doctor or D.O., Doctor of Osteopathy.

In the 60's each state developed its own laws and examination system to test applicants seeking architectural licensure. Architects licensed in one state desiring to do work in another state would apply for "reciprocity", meaning the two state's examination and legal systems would be compared for compatibility to allow transportability of one's architectural practice, sometimes requiring some added testing. That compatibility was at times difficult to determine and so a national board, NCARB, the National Council of Architectural Registration Boards, was formed to expedite the comparison process.

ME THE DAY I
GOT MY
REGISTRATION

ME NOW

ARCHITECTURE TAKES ALOT OUT OF YOU —
BUT IT PUTS BACK IN MORE THAN IT TAKES.

THERE IS AN OLD JOKE WHICH HAPPENS TO
BE TOO CLOSE TO TRUTH " THE BEST WAY TO
MAKE A SMALL FORTUNE IN ARCHITECTURE
IS TO START OUT WITH A LARGE FORTUNE."

Unfortunately, like all national boards, the NCARB has gravitated to the development of a standard national test that will eventually replace individual state tests. The rationale is that the individual state exams are not consistent – DUH – requiring the NCARB to provide resolution to achieve compatibility, which was their original charge.

In my opinion replacing individual state examinations with a single national exam is not a good idea. Each state is concerned that architects have special design knowledge for local physical conditions such as earthquakes, severe freezing or heat, violent winds or flooding, as well as knowledge of local codes and restrictions. Expecting that a single exam can do an adequate job of covering all possible conditions is unrealistic. Why would an architect living and practicing in Hawaii need to know about falling ice hazards, or should an architect in Kansas know about shoreline erosion control?

About the Hawaiian architect, I was wondering where Hawaiians go to relax?

In 1964 I got my license to practice architecture by passing the State of Arizona Architectural Registration Exam, sans degree. Having a degree meant nothing to me. A degree does not allow you to practice architecture, a license does. Which would you rather have? The day my license certificate arrived in the mail I quit my job and opened my practice in my storage room, shared with the water heater and gardening equipment. A bit cramped, but the price was right.

One of my first clients, apparently tired of squeezing into my "office", offered free vacant space in a building he was trying to sell with the agreement that I would begin paying rent or move out when he sold the building. I called a friend, Miles Stahm, who was contemplating starting his own practice and offered to share the free rent. We each proudly put our signs in the window: "Nick Devenney, Architect" and "Miles Stahm, Architect". Within two weeks we were referred to as "Devenney and Stahm, Architects", a happy mistake that lasted for eighteen years. Miles and I made great partners, and remain great friends.

The early years were a learning process. Discovering how to run a business instead of an atelier was necessary to support our habits of eating, having a car, a house, etc. – running a design studio is the dream, running a business is a reality.

After eighteen years Miles decided to concentrate on smaller highly personalized projects and I wanted to push for larger more complex work, so we amicably parted and I launched Devenney Associates, Ltd., DAL, without associates at the time, but it sounded good. Later, DAL would spawn Devenney Group, Ltd., Architects, DGL; Project Development Resources, Ltd., PDR; and Project Construction Resources, PCR.

DAL and its subsequent subsidiaries have for years been solely focused on the design of facilities that provide healthcare, especially hospitals. I trust that physicians and hospital administrators will read this with an open mind, and a sense of humor. If not, stop now to help reduce the volume of hate mail I might receive.

The biggest business mistake young architects, (and a lot of old ones too), make is not making a business plan.

I offer mine that worked exceedingly well for forty-five years, a simple four step model:

1. **Find the work**
2. **Do the work**
3. **Collect the money**
4. **Repeat**

Sneer away, MBA wonks – it works! Some business management guru coined the catchy phrase "You can't manage what you can't measure", and made a fortune on the speaker's circuit and book royalties. Well, for those of you who have drunk the management by metrics Kool-Aid, let me simplify things. The metric that is most important in my four step model is Step #1, because if it fails there is no reason to worry about #2 and 3, and you won't have a chance to do #4.

It also helps to focus on a particular category of buildings and become expert in all the special needs of those buildings. Additionally become expert in the businesses that occupy the buildings. For me it was medical facilities. By the '80s we were almost totally focused on facilities for healthcare, predominantly hospitals.

Marketing is not just an important part of your practice. It is your practice. Contrary to what you learned in school, commissions are not won with slick photos of cool buildings you did for other people – clients want an architect that can custom design their project. Issues such as your fee, how you will meet schedules and budgets, etc. are of course important to them, but they assume these issues can be resolved between friends. Yes, friends. It is important that they view your firm as a friendly partner, not as an instructor. It is important that they like you. Conversely, it is important that you like them. If your instincts sense they are potentially not a good fit with your firm's culture, evaluate just how badly you need the job.

The following excerpt is from one of my many memos to staff in which I try to emphasize where our work comes from. It is not from our architecture, it is from our relationships.

> We talk a lot about the importance of project management. It is very important. But even more important is client relationship management.
>
> Good project management includes managing our client, developing relationships that hopefully continue long after a project is completed.
>
> Our ability to obtain future work depends almost entirely on our client relationships – referrals, references and reputation – rather than photos and awards for the buildings...

That's why we need to begin increasing our focus on client relationships. "Losing a client" is much more damaging than "losing a project". If we compete for a project we currently do not have and are not successful in obtaining it we erroneously say we "lost" the project – <u>the project we never had</u>. However, if we lose a client, <u>we lose something we had, something of great value</u>.

You see my drift – that our clients are more important than "our" projects. The word "our" is in quotes because it is the first big mistake often made – the projects are <u>not ours</u>, they <u>belong to the client</u>. This is not just semantic quibbling.

When meeting with user groups, administration, physicians, facility management etc. it is important that we communicate with them in ways they want to hear.

- ➤ *Confirmation that they are in control, not us.*
- ➤ *It is their meeting, not ours.*
- ➤ *Their ideas are advanced for us to execute as best we can, not offered for critique or change.*
- ➤ *They recognize we know more about architecture than they do. They want us to acknowledge that they know more about healthcare and how they want to provide it than we do.*
- ➤ *They want information and performance from us on the schedule they require – no exceptions.*

> *They like the Marine Corp service standard –*
> *"No excuse, sir!"*
> *Just because they own the building they want lots of control over how it looks. How presumptuous.*

Whether you like it or not, _being liked is more important than being right, creative, or competent in maintenance of client relationships._

Assume two competing architects, X and Z, are interviewing for a project. Architect X clearly has more experience and the ego to go with it. Architect Z has less experience, but is a likeable gal. Most times Z will win. Why? Selection committees consider that they are selecting a design partner, not a teacher, and the relationship is going to go on for several years – for hospital projects. So who would they rather deal with over the long haul? The one they like best.

The void in an architect's brain that should be occupied with business knowledge has a significant empty pocket labeled "time management". We are poor time managers because we assume projects can be done in unrealistic timeframes – and commit to them – and, more importantly, we don't know how to stop. There is always one more option to explore. There is no such thing as the final solution. Also, no matter how much we complain, what we do is very absorbing and enjoyable. The euphoria of beginning one's own practice coupled with being completely unaware of the implications of the phrase "time is money" sow the seeds of bad business practices that sprout for decades.

Few architects are good at marketing in part because they don't like and/or understand it, believing it is selling, or competing, etc. For a group that is basically risk averse, non competitive, has a low tolerance for criticism or rejection, and thinks "selling" is unprofessional – it is not a shock that they do not make good marketers.

To make matters worse, architects are generally poor business managers. They see quantitative management by metrics as an easy option rather than a management with a holistic view of the practice, value comparisons rather than metric equation, and common sense.

Architects think of themselves as "problem seekers" which means design problems, not business problems. Actually their penchant for seeking problems is one of the most critical business management problems in an architectural practice – designers never stop seeking, every solution presents interesting options, and the design clock runs amok, (what is "amok"?), a time management discussion for later.

I recently did some consulting for an architectural practice consisting of about twenty shareholder employees plus forty or so non-shareholder employees. This firm is a poster child for what can happen to a firm that depends on management by metrics instead of leadership by intuition and common sense. Metrics provided a clear certainty of where they have been, and a vague guess as to where they are going. Metrics convey data having no context.

The firm's management had a morbid intense focus on metrics that showed a declining revenue curve. Their solution: balance it out by altering the expense curve via formula and metrics. By example making up lists of employees to be gradually terminated as revenues declined. Inexplicably (to me) several shareholder employees were on the list. Reason? In management's recent productivity evaluations some shareholders scored lower (slightly and debatably) than some non-shareholders performing similar roles. Here is an example of a solution in search of an application with complete ignorance of critical decision consequences (because metrics don't show such things) that could potentially cripple the firm's ability to survive. A few examples:

1. Firing a shareholder would have negative economic consequences such as buying back their stock.
2. One could expect a shareholder would, for loyalty and economic reasons, be likely to stick around through hard times, versus a non-owner employee who may well jump ship when things look bad.
3. If a shareholder (in which the firm has made an investment) scores low on a metric evaluation, how about leadership stepping in with additional investments like better mentoring, education etc. instead of canning them.
4. Firing ownership has got to send extremely negative messages to the troops that things are critical and maybe they should get out the resumes.

5.   Firing selected members of their ownership group also would have negative unintended consequences among the shareholders who probably (hopefully) have developed strong personal as well as professional and business bonds

Just the message the firm needs from management – panic!

Scenario: An owner employee who is not quite as capable as formidable Frank, a non-owner employee, is terminated. Three weeks later formidable Frank, sensing management's panic, leaves for more stable pastures. What an insightful solution to declining revenues.

If the firm has a non-performing shareholder, I would think an increased attention to helping that individual to be "all they can be" in lieu of firing them would be good management. If they have reached their maximum capabilities, then assign them to responsibilities that match their abilities, and adjust their pay scale accordingly. It is a dumb expectation that all shareholders will be equal and will progress at the same pace.

Certainly tightening the belt is a critical step to take in declining revenues, and payroll is a fat target. But – leadership must have faith that revenues will improve (if they don't then its time to fire everyone, cut losses, and nail the door shut) and when revenues improve it will be because of increased workload which will need the very employees (and owners) being fired to get the work out, quickly followed by revenue generating invoices.

There is a saying in all agricultural societies similar to "Don't eat your seed corn". Your key people are your seed corn for future crops.

Maintaining the firm's productivity capability should be a high priority. Some solutions could include maybe all owners taking a temporary reduction in salary, or putting hourly staff on a thirty-five hour week, or temporarily reducing salaried folks. How about doing work for valued clients at cost – even below cost – to try to stimulate projects going forward (revenue), and to help keep staff together. Go the extra mile: <u>no</u> charge! Even doing <u>free</u> work is better than doing <u>no</u> work, if you believe in the firm's ability to increase revenues and stay in business. <u>Doing nothing will generate nothing</u>.
Metrics make sense when applied to quantitative issues such as finance. But metrics are relatively useless for measuring qualitative issues, either retrospectively, (did the artist do a good painting), or prospectively, (how much is the painting worth).

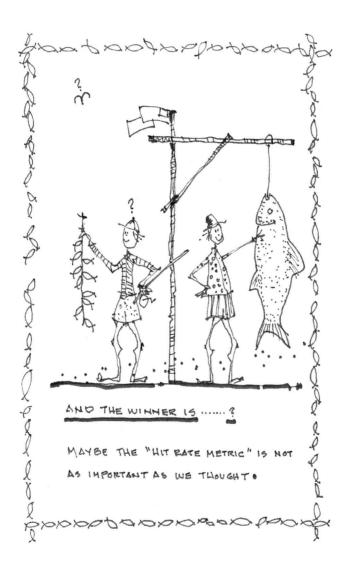

AND THE WINNER IS ....?

MAYBE THE "HIT RATE METRIC" IS NOT
AS IMPORTANT AS WE THOUGHT.

Metrics have real value for some things – but not all. Unfortunately they are often used as an "easy" way to manage, but they are a poor substitute for leadership.

By example, firms often use metrics to track their "hit rate" for success at chasing RFPs. I think the national average is something like 15%. Doesn't matter. Say you respond to ten RFPs that randomly range from a fee of $500,000 to $10,000,000 you get two – a 20% hit rate · wow! Unfortunately, you got the two lowest fee jobs, so are you a success? Maybe tracking the total fee dollars in a years worth of RFPs and seeing what percentage of the fees you got might be more instructive than how many RFP projects you got.

Another warning signal to watch for is what the Harvard Business Review refers to as the "Narcissism Index" in management which tracks the use of first person singular in discussing company issues, such as "I plan to do XX" in lieu of "we should do XX". An erosion of the concept of **WE** will signal that people are believing that if they are responsible for a department they can unilaterally make decisions for that department without understanding that the firm is a collaborative.

Which brings me to the core of the discussion. To paraphrase a political campaign slogan – "It's the marketing stupid". That should be the major topic for discussion at leadership meetings. It is not the declining revenue curve but the W.A.G. (wild ass guess) curve – a best guess prediction of projects the firm may get during the next two or three years that bears watching. A decline in the W.A.G. curve will cause a corresponding decline in revenues about twelve months later. Message: kick marketing's ass.

Marketing is the most vital metric management should watch, but other things like bar charts for employee satisfaction surveys, performance evaluations, productivity measurements, cash on hand, etc. seems to be more interesting; probably because they are formula based and supposedly have some certainty. The subjective intelligence summarized in a "wild ass guess" is thought to be too esoteric pie in the sky stuff to be reliable. News flash, metric lovers. It's the <u>only</u> "metric" that keeps a firm going. Without it you won't need to worry about a revenue curve because there soon won't be any.

In addition to being poor business people nobody ever accused architects of being good negotiators. Our work is grossly undervalued compared to other project participants. The following letter to the editors of the Phoenix Business Journal tried to make a wry yet accurate commentary on a situation wherein I took one of my clients to a building to lease space for a new practice I was to design for him. I thought it interesting that the leasing agent I delivered my physician client to got a leasing commission that exceeded my fee for design and engineering. Another lesson learned a little late.

From the Phoenix Business Journal, September 8, 1995.

MANY ARE PUTTING COST OVER VALUE

Dear Editor:

Your article on architectural fees ("Firms seek to bid farewell to old fee basis" by D.J. Burrough, August 18) spotlights a very critical issue not only for architectural businesses, but our entire business system as well – an increasing assumption that cost is more important than value. In a society that pays its garbage collectors more than its teachers, I suppose this trend should not be surprising, albeit alarming.

I have enclosed a "sanitized" copy of a letter (reprinted below) I recently sent to one of our clients regarding architectural fees. While drafted with tongue-in-cheek, it nonetheless points out the relative value of services between negotiating a tenant lease versus providing architectural services impacting the total project safety, cost, functionality, beauty, operational efficiency, resale value, financiability, etc.

Thanks for highlighting a very critical problem in our "comparative-analysis" addicted business system. Unfortunately it is much easier for a business manager to "compare" quantitative data – fees – instead of qualitative data – value.

Nick Devenney
President
Devenney Associates, Ltd., Architects

June 12, 1995
Phoenix, AZ

Re: Mesa Project

Messrs: _____

I have been thinking of ways to establish the professional fee DAL will charge for the project and have decided the most fair and equitable way is to make the architectural fee consistent with other professional fees being charged to the project.

As a benchmark I have used your leasing agent's fee of $50,000 for his efforts in leasing the building which I have not yet designed. Since you have included this fee in the project cost without question or reduction, I assume $50,000 is a fair fee for the amount of time and liability – not to mention expertise – the leasing agent will expend in the interest of the project.

Since the DAL staff and I will be expending well over ten times the hours as the leasing agent spent, it appears an architectural fee of $500,000 is more than fair, assuming an equal level of liability, and that the expertise required to lease the building is the same as that required to design the building.

Of course, unlike Mr. _____, we will need extensive consultant assistance (structural, civil, mechanical, electrical, and plumbing engineering, etc.) to provide our work. We will ask our engineers to similarly establish their fees using the leasing fee as a benchmark. As a professional courtesy we will pass those fees through to you with no mark-up.

Upon acceptance of our contract and fee, we will prepare the design of the project. I am sure everyone associated with the project is anxiously awaiting our work to be completed since without it not much can be established, like how big is the building; is the site usable; how much does it cost and therefore what lease rate; how long will it take; what does it look like; how leased spaces are designed; what will be special city requirements; generation of a project appraisal; obtaining a mortgage commitment; structuring a project pro forma; determining if earth be imported or exported; how utilities will be accessed, etc., etc.

I know these issues sound trivial but they are our small contribution to the project which may help others understand the scope of their respective, more important, roles and tasks.

Very truly yours,
Nick Devenney

<u>Unfortunately some things never change</u>.

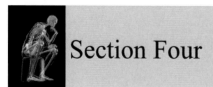

Section Four

While we are into old letters, the following is a letter to a good friend who is an expert in healthcare journalism. Even though it is now very old, it occurred to me it might still have current relevance.

August 1, 1995

Ms. Angela Gonzales
The Business Journal
2910 North Central Ave.
Phoenix, AZ 85012-2704

Dear Angela,
Here are a few thoughts for your article on healthcare.

If Washington concentrated on controlling the insurance industry and disease prevention instead of the health care industry and disease treatment, reasonable health care cost and universal coverage could begin to be achieved.

If the Feds required insurance companies to offer policies having premiums based upon a national instead of individual policy holder experience, more stable and reasonable premiums could be obtained. Also policies should not be subject to selective cancellation or premium increases, unless all policy holders under the same plan are uniformly treated.

Employers would be much more inclined to purchase employee insurance if premiums could not be raised if an employee became severely ill, or the policy cancelled because the insurance company decides the employees had become a bad risk.

Disease prevention should be administered by the Government because such programs don't make immediate profits and are therefore unpopular with private industry. Mandatory national programs for vaccinations, pre-natal care, nutrition, health screening, etc. would produce a population requiring less frequent and less costly treatment.

Since prevention programs would directly benefit insurance companies, it would not be unreasonable to expect them to provide substantial financial and/or administrative support for such programs, shifting part of the burden from taxpayers

There must be some control mechanism either via the insurance industry or the Feds to set acceptable ratios for premiums vs. claims, e.g. 80% of premiums paid to claims or, said another way, a cap on administrative costs and profits as a percentage of revenue. Multimillion dollar *administrative insurance salaries seem out of synch with the value of the folks who actually provide care...*

It is understandable that insurance companies choose not to offer coverage to individuals having costly existing medical conditions. A federal subsidy to cover premium costs above standard insurance rates plus requirements that no one can be declined coverage would permit such individuals to be included in the private system, instead of the entire cost of the "uninsurable" being borne by the taxpayers.

If private insurance providers do not address these issues, some form of federal provider system will do so. If a national effort to control unnecessary disease and disability through prevention measures is not soon implemented, unnecessary costs and burden to the health care industry will continue to escalate.

America already has a very efficient health care insurance system in place which only needs federal assistance or coercion, to make it more effective and stable. And if the federal government used its power to provide prevention programs a more healthy population base could be achieved.

Best regards,

Nick Devenney, A.I.A.
President

Devenney Associates, Ltd.

Sometimes oldies are goodies. It pays to never throw away ideas or clothes because sooner or later they come back in style.

As I write this President Obama is advancing his agenda for healthcare. By the time you read this he will or will not have been successful, so discussion about his plan is pointless. Apparently the "reform" is primarily for the insurance industry, not healthcare. The issue should be cheaper and better healthcare, like eliminating the cost of the 15% of Medicare expenditures that are fraudulent, or reducing the incidence of sepsis that currently kills 48,000 per year at the cost of 8 billion dollars. Whatever the purpose of "Healthcare Reform" we are told its legislation must be past ASAP, and don't worry if there are little hiccups in it that don't work, they can be fixed later.

Tocquieville discussed "do over's" in the making of laws: "The most perilous moment for a bad government is one when it seeks to mend its ways."

I am hoping things like allowing competing private health insurance companies to sell on a national basis instead of only intra state, providing policies without exclusions, and a cap on profits and senior compensation is a part of the system. And that the Feds reimburse hospitals for the actual cost of care instead of an arbitrary reduced amount which forces hospitals to "cost shift" (the origin of the gripes about five dollar aspirins) so that they can cling to their whopping 1.5% profit margin.

Also maybe bringing sanity to tort reform and the "defensive medicine" practices it causes would also be an easy fix by changing laws, which probably won't happen because Congress is populated with, ‑ guess what ‑ lawyers. Tort laws are state laws, so the Fed can't directly change them but, as the old Nazi films say, "We have ways".

Legal settlements for the value of the loss of a life or a limb can be measured by insurance amortization systems. Unfortunately the value of "pain and suffering" and "quality of life" issues can't be measured, so settlement amounts are left up to juries who are generally partial to "sticking it to the insurance company", that faceless owner of large gobs of free money. For a skillful lawyer with a pitiable (and well coached) client this system is a pathway to early retirement. It is also the pathway to higher healthcare cost. Before you bitch about what the hospitals charge ask yourself if you would like to own a hospital with all its phenomenal risks just to <u>maybe</u> make a 1.5% profit?

>*Bulletin: A small boy swallowed some coins and the hospital kept him for observation. When his mother called to ask how he was the nurse said there was no change yet.*

Of course the problem isn't what hospitals charge so much as what hospitals spend. That's at least a four volume set I may someday write. Just don't lay it on the architects – the mortgage payment for our stuff is only a very small part of a hospital's annual operational costs.

The population sometimes can get lathered up about a new hospital that "looks expensive", and assume the architect spent all the hospital's money on fancy lobbies instead of decent sized patient rooms. Well yes, they are right – more about such disproportionate space values later. However the cost of the mortgage payments on hospital buildings does not amount to much – three percent or less of annual expenses. Ninety-seven percent of expense is attributable to what happens after the building opens, most of it payroll.

Another thing contributing to hospital cost is complying with an avalanche of regulation. The only industry more highly regulated than hospitals is nuclear power. Of course the nuclear power industry does not kill over 250,000 people per year by mistake, like hospitals do.

Maybe regulation is good. Or maybe regulations adhered to is what is needed. Something is wrong and it is not the architecture.

I don't think the hospital's architecture contributes to many patient deaths; however we architects have been accused of killing polar bears and flooding beach resorts. Yes, global warming. The construction industry (and we architects are complicit with it) is a veritable ecological destruction machine. Consider what construction does: emits 30% of the CO2, and 40% of the sulfur dioxide and also consumes 40% of the world's energy, 40% of non-renewable minerals, 25% of virgin wood, and 16% of our water supply.

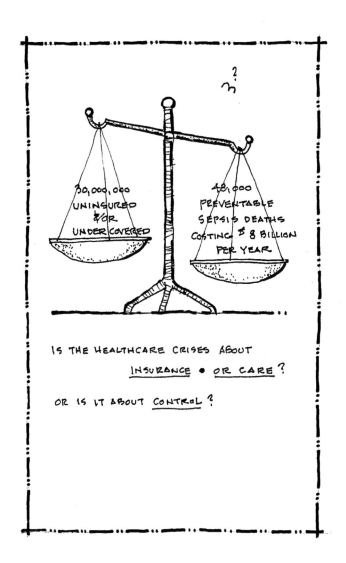

IS THE HEALTHCARE CRISES ABOUT
              INSURANCE • OR CARE?

OR IS IT ABOUT CONTROL?

Wasteful little buggers, aren't we? An entire consulting profession has sprung up to battle our dismal record – LEED, "Leadership in Energy and Environmental Design", - dedicated to helping architecture contribute to sustainability. A laudable goal but difficult to define. What does "sustainability" mean? Sustain what, for whom, and for how long? And at what cost?

Somehow the concepts of sustainability and global warming have become intertwined. Since global warming seems to be the most immediate concern let's discuss it first.

Current Armageddon stories about sustainability seem to generate a proper sense of crises that can stampede public acceptance of commitments that may not be achievable, let alone sustainable. There is nothing like ringing an alarm bell to get people moving. In the early '70s Paul Ehrlich's books scared the kaka out of us all by predicting that by the mid '80s the world would run out of food.

To borrow a hackneyed phrase from our president, "First, let me make myself clear" - I do believe that the earth is gradually warming. I also believe humans are capable of mitigating the damage that may cause and I believe doing so will require selfless dedication to goals only realized after our death. I additionally believe humans have a spotty record for embracing such dedication. Most importantly I believe there are immediate issues that pose a more dire threat to humanity and the planet than warming – such as North Korea and Iran as nuclear powers. Ebola virus becoming airborne or a worldwide shortage of chocolate.

That's a lot of " I believes", but I'm sticking to them. A photo of a drowned polar bear is a real attention grabber. My God, they are already disappearing! But what about reality as reported by Bjorn Lomorg in his book _Cool It?_ Mr. Lomborg points out that out of twenty subpopulations of polar bears possibly two are reducing. However, on a global basis the bear population has increased from around five-thousand in the 60's to twenty-five thousand today.

I have read a theory that humans have reached such a nadir of perfection that we are, on purpose and, inadvertently, directing evolution. Maybe that was a misprint, "directing" instead of "destroying". Our chutzpah never ends. We should be lucky if some microscopic wiggle worm virus doesn't decide to do a little evolutionary engineering of its own and wipes us off the earth.

Lomborg also points out that the images of people drowning in their own sweat with thousands dying of heat stroke may be overblown. More people die from cold each year than from heat. Currently in Europe 200,000 people die from heat per year, and 1,500,000 die from cold. A 7½ to one ratio. It is projected that a 3.6 degree increase in global temperature will kill 2,000 more people per year, but it will save 20,000 deaths from cold. Maybe 18,000 saved lives is a good thing but when discussing sustainability it is obvious that relative to the metrics of human population, the architectural adage of "less is more" is a more useful goal.

Apparently 98% of all the species of animals that have ever lived are already extinct. Anybody miss them?

"Sustainability: to keep in existence or prolong."
Webster.

How long is prolong? And prolong what? The planet?
Or an optimal quality of life for humans?

Defining sustainability requires making major
assumptions about the future. Such as population
growth and dispersment, or technological advances.
Natural disasters. Human disasters, aka nuclear war.
Most studies seem to assume current trends will
continue at least through the foreseeable future. My
crystal ball is fuzzy.

> *Notice:: A short fortune teller has escaped from
> prison. A bulletin has been issued to watch out
> for a small medium at large.*

We must assume all subsequent generations will
willingly and diligently meet the commitments of the
sustainability plans we devise today, otherwise our yap
yap about saving the earth is meaningless.

> *"Individual interests are the only real interests...
> Can it be conceived that there are men so absurd
> as to prefer the man, who is not, to him who is; to
> torment the living under presence of promoting
> the happiness of those who are not born, and
> may never be born?"*
> *Jeremy Bentham, 1843*

Well yes, there are men so absurd.

A discussion about sustainability must start with an agreement regarding what is to be sustained, for whom, and for how long. I assume the "what" and "how long" depends on the "whom". If the "what" refers to those elements of the physical environment necessary to maintain a healthy and productive life cycle for the "whom", then identification of the "whom" is critical, because the definition of a sustainable environment differs greatly among the "whoms" – redwood trees, e-coli bacteria, lemurs, cod, plankton, elephants, house flies, etc. and of course, the chosen life form of the universe, humans. Perhaps we are the chosen because we are the only ones who are aware that a future is coming, and have the ability to worry about it.

Unfortunately we humans are the only life form that seeks to sustain <u>not only a life *cycle*, but also a life *style*</u>, consisting of a rapidly increasing array of "things" assumed to be an indispensable part of life and living large. Skis, autos, violins, TVs, ad infinitum are considered by humans to be as important as life itself. Indeed, we are willing to kill for them, if someone tries to steal them from us.

If sustainability is defined as "for humans", it then becomes much more complex because we must be able to sustain not just our lives, but the production and maintenance of the things that are <u>not necessary *for*</u> our life but that we believe <u>we must have *in*</u> our life.

These "things" are neither naturally occurring nor self replicating. Their creation is dependent upon conversion of elements of the natural environment into unnatural artifacts, like cannons or condoms. Actually, two products that can greatly assist sustainability!

The sustainability discussion then becomes not only how to insure that our species can sustain life, but more importantly how to feed our limitless need for more things. Sustaining our life <u>cycle</u> requires little environmental intrusion compared to sustaining our life <u>style</u> which requires massive environmental destruction.

Advocates for environmental sustainability are setting goals that our generation must achieve to meet our self imposed duty to insure current levels of environmental assets and resources will be available to future generations, with "future" being an unspecified metric. There is an apt Chinese proverb: "One generation plants the trees, future generations enjoy the shade".

This system of beliefs is sometimes referred to as our "environmental legacy" for those yet to come. A legacy of an *intact physical environment* is laudable, but a *successful social environment* of tolerance, freedom, safety and mutual respect might be a more useful legacy, and probably more appreciated.

If as much rhetoric and energy were devoted to saving ourselves from ourselves, instead of saving the planet from ourselves, we might evolve a much more valuable gift for the folks in 2999 and beyond.
Insuring a <u>higher</u> living standard for potential future populations at the expense of many who are alive today seems unjust at best. Spending today's energies and

assets to raise current standards of living, to increase health and education, to eradicate the potential for a nuclear or pandemic Armageddon, in short doing things today that will enhance the standard of living in the future, may be more appreciated in the future.

The term "sustainable" is meaningless without the metrics of time and volumes, i.e., sustainable for how long, and at what rate of consumption. Evidently Mars once had abundant water. It is now a dry planet. If humans had lived there 500,000 years ago could they ‑ should they have saved Mars' water asset for our generation? In a long view we may be overestimating our abilities as controlling guardians of the planet.

Environmental assets are usually defined as either non‑renewable or renewable. Apparently those classified as non‑renewable assets are most troublesome because by definition, if used at all, they will run out, at which point generations beyond the date of their depletion are out of assets. Accordingly, sustainability is not a concept without end. It is a concept to forestall the end, sustaining assets for as long a period of time as possible, but not indefinitely.

If we can identify the period of time for which we must plan, and then calculate the average number of consuming humans to be alive during that period, and then determine the current volume of reserves of non‑renewable assets, we can set an annual per capita consumption quota for non‑renewable assets like oil. Two factors of this equation are fixed – time and asset volume. Therefore the rate of depletion depends on the number of humans to be accommodated – assuming technology will not change over time. Of course it will.

By example, ten thousand years ago our ancestors gathered dried animal feces to burn as a primary energy source. They could not imagine nuclear power. Ten thousand years from now our animal feces equivalent – oil – will be replaced by something we cannot now image. Maybe like sun plus magnifying glass equals heat plus water equals steam plus engine equals electricity?

It seems odd that the species of fauna that is most environmentally destructive considers it their duty to first preserve their own species, and second to meter the destruction they cause over as long a period of time as possible. Humans contribute absolutely nothing to the environment except, as all living things do, upon death donate back to the earth the insignificant package of minerals and chemicals we fondly call our bodies. It is ironic that humans consider themselves the savior of the earth while the best thing that could happen to the earth would be for all of us to disappear.

There are several steps towards finding a way to balance our rate of plunder with the earth's ability to recover. First, reduce the population. Lots of luck. First we must overcome various churches, societal mores and a medical profession intent on battling Mother Nature's efforts to thin the herd.

In his book "*Hot, Flat & Crowded*" Thomas Friedman presents many ingenious suggestions for mitigation of global warming and other destabilizing influences on the environment. By example Friedman notes that a worldwide total elimination of all forms of motorized transportation would reduce carbon emissions by only 14%. Makes increasing my gas mileage by 5 mpg seem like a futile effort. It is.

I just read that several cities in California are replacing their public transportation buses with new natural gas powered more earth friendly models. California is on the verge of bankruptcy. The bus changeover will be costly and amount to a spit in the ocean for saving the earth. But it makes everyone all warm and fuzzy that "we are doing something positive", although it is positively ineffective for the climate, and positively destructive to the financial condition of the town. Multiply this lunacy by 10,000 and you begin to understand why sustainability may be a difficult goal.

One of the most telling points in Friedman's book is made via a quote from Chevron's CEO, David O'Reilly that brings energy consumption versus availability into focus. He calculates the world's current daily consumption of energy expressed as oil indicates we are currently consuming <u>ten million barrels *per hour*</u>.

Right now, our standard of living is enjoyed by a billion people, and there is an additional two billion getting close.

But there are over three billion more people who want to move up but can't for many reasons. And there will be another three billion born within forty years.

So you can see our energy supply today, ten million barrels per hour, just meets the needs of three billion lucky folks.

To serve the existing unlucky three billion who need to move up, plus accommodate the three billion who are arriving on the stork express, we will need to triple our energy consumption if we don't make drastic changes. This will give you a hint about the possible unsustainability of sustainability: as the number of humans increase the possible duration of sustainability decreases.
Doesn't the problem make the primary solution obvious?
Fewer people.

There is a theory that the birth rate will naturally decline through sociological changes rather than biological restraint. Supposedly as women in an emerging society become better educated, discover contraception, and become employed outside the home they will have fewer babies, thereby reducing the birth rate. This condition is referred to as a decline in the "fertility rate", aka the pregnancy rate, and is advanced as Mother Nature's way of controlling runaway baby booms.

Reduction in the fertility rate only occurs after a higher standard of living is achieved for women either by forces such as China's one child law, or by a slow evolution of a society from a system of people having eight kids hoping at least two survive to take care of them in their old age, or to a government care system such as social security, or a Gulag.

It is true that the more technologically advanced a society becomes the fewer people it requires to produce the goods and services to support it. No longer are all of the people required to work all of the time just to maintain a food supply plus the artifacts of civilization that we need, or want. At that point we should slow down the baby machine. Unfortunately we don't. Political, religious, economic and limbic influences seem to keep the machine going.

Tom Malthus was right in 1798: *"Population, when unchecked, increases in a geometrical ratio. Subsistence increases only in arithmetical ratio".*

The idea that the entire population need not work to produce our food and products brings up an interesting conundrum. Work is society's mechanism for distributing money to individuals. But what if a percentage of the population does not have to work, doesn't have a job? How do they get money? AH! Socialism, with a guaranteed minimum income. I like the fewer people scenario better. Unfortunately a recent study in Denmark predicts people born since 2000 have a "reasonable" life expectancy of 100+ years. Without a decline in birth rates or a pandemic plague this is not good news for sustainability.

The sustainability dream can possibly come true via the old architectural mantra <u>less is more</u> - less people with more responsible consumerism. We should produce products needed to enhance health, welfare, education, etc. – items necessary for the good of our species. We must also reduce the rate and scope of manufacturing things just because we can, or just because we want them. We should make things primarily because we need them. This suggestion blunts our cherished belief in the necessity for continuous product improvement, innovation and invention – bigger, faster, stronger, etc. These are the engines that drive our economic system and destroys our ecological system.

Products whose sole purpose is to provide a variety of personal choices or non-essential activities must eventually be limited. How many varieties of vacuum cleaners or cell phones do we need? Jet skies are fun, but are they ecologically worth it? Especially if everyone on earth should have the ability to own one. Nine billion of them and counting?

Our damaging ecological impact has been not only by voracious consumption of earth's assets, but by consuming them in a disposable form. We have invented a process that removes our guilt – recycling – by assuming no damage to the environment occurs if a new car is made by recycling an old car. Our passion for plastic as a throw away container may itself eventually strangle our systems.

I guess we are ready to accept some level of pollution as being acceptable rather than reducing it by any means possible within economic reality. Have you heard about "pollute and swap", otherwise known as "cap and trade"? It works like this. Say I have a factory that is pumping out ten tons of carbon a day, and to put filters on my facility will cost me five million dollars plus production disruption for five years. But wait! I can go to my neighborhood carbon broker and buy carbon credits from some guy in South America who owns a tree farm that absorbs ten tons of carbon per day. Buying credits (credits = a pass to pollute) from the tree farmer is cheaper than fixing my factory. So I save money, the tree farmer makes money, everybody is happy, and my factory is still dumping ten tons a day! I'm still trying to figure out how pollution is reduced. Who checks to make sure the trees haven't died?

I don't believe constantly increasing more product choices to a constantly expanding population is a sustainable process. But it is the process we have chosen and evolved. We did it because we want our way, we want it now, and we are not going to give it up.

Currently there is a finger pointing fracas about whether certain climate studies are valid, or worse yet misleading. Some argue that sustainability issues are no longer important because of flawed science. Could be. But the true believers cling to what has become known as the "precautionary principle" formulated in the early '90s by the UN Economic Conference for Europe which states in part: "In order to achieve sustainable development, policies must be based on the precautionary principal.... Where there are threats of serious or irreversible damage, lack of full scientific certainty should not be used as a reason for postponing measures to prevent environmental degradation." So just do it whether you know if it's needed or not, or if it will work or not.

Saving the earth has become our latest crises movement. It's a good thing. We should curb waste and keep our nest tidy. But like all movements, this one has moved too far when it tries to predict and protect conditions far into the uncontrollable future.

It's like we are at a party with a small punch bowl. If the party requires punch to exist, then everyone must drink in moderation to make the party last as long as possible. But eventually the punch <u>will</u> run out. I think we will party till the punch is gone, hoping it will last forever.

> *Bulletin:* It has been reported someone has bored a hole through the nudist colony fence. The police are looking into it.

Concepts of time depend on a point of view, by example:

> *A turtle was strolling through a garden one day and was mugged by three snails. When the police arrived they asked the turtle if he could describe the assailants, to which he replied, "Oh my goodness, No! You see, it all happened so fast!"*

Another example:

> *The aquatic mayfly lives its entire life in less than a day. A human day. Mayflies evidently have short "to do" lists.*

LARRY AND PEEWEE

Section Five

Well, now that saving the planet for people in the future is complete, we can move on to other more important issues – stuff that will affect <u>us</u> while <u>we</u> are alive. Making a living, doing good things, understanding, loving, creating, stuff like that, while keeping an eye on the other guy to be sure he does unto you as you would have him believe you would do unto him.

One of my current "doing untos" involves a relationship that has developed between Larry and me. Larry spends a good deal of time worrying about sustainability. His. Larry has no home, and few belongings, except a bottomless well of love called Peewee, a chiwawa – hell you try to spell it! Larry and Peewee sit quietly by a restaurant I frequent. They do not beg. They are an obvious living statement that some of us have a better life than others. The reasons why Larry is in this condition have no meaning. Larry and Peewee need help, and in small ways I can help provide it. Larry's current major problem is the Phoenix July heat. He cannot escape it, 24/7. No place cool will welcome him, or more precisely, Peewee. They make quick tours of the supermarkets, the library, etc. but soon Larry is asked to leave because of "no dogs allowed policies". Homeless shelters will welcome Larry for a cool night indoors, but not Peewee, citing health codes. There is no way Larry will leave Peewee.

I believe what Larry experiences in being turned away from stores and restaurants is resistance to how he is dressed, not Peewee. If Larry wore cool looking golf duds and Peewee was a white fuzz ball with a rhinestone collar they could get in anywhere. But he doesn't have cool looking duds, and it's hard to look sharp when you are in 110 degree heat 24 hours a day. Larry and I are asking the shelters if we got some carry cages donated if they would allow them to be placed inside overnight for homeless person's pets.

Peewee is not just a dog. As Larry told me, "This little guy is the only thing that loves me now". "Now" is the crushing word in that sentence, telling me that there was a time of love for Larry, now gone.

What caused such devastation, an event that drained all confidence and hope out of a person I am sure was once a proud and talented man, left clutching for dear life to the only thing he believes loves him? I presume God loves him, unless He is that vengeful God we hear about and Larry has pissed Him off. So Peewee is "it" for Larry. The irony is that any dog would gladly fill in for Peewee. That is the mission of dogs, to provide love without judgment of any kind, patiently sharing whatever hardships their human companion must endure.

I was given a dog when I was a small boy and named it Prince. I must have been quite small because later in life I grew to realize Prince should have been named Princess, but by any name there never was a dog that loved its master more. She waited patiently for years while I was gone, and knew all my hurts when I returned. She would lie on top of me at night and cry with me. She could literally smile when happy. She felt my every feeling. Through the years she grew ever more feeble, reaching some 18 years before some monstrous cruelty of nature began a terminal pain deep inside.

I put off the inevitable, hoping some miracle might occur. Late one night I awoke and found her, laying on the kitchen floor near her water dish, faintly whimpering. She could not rise, and gave me a look with deep brown eyes that made me know. I carried her to the Vet and held her tightly as the needle went in, felt her recoil, and then a final resting. She never took her eyes off mine. I buried her in the back yard. I thought it would be the most difficult act of my life. I was wrong.

Well the point of this digression is not about dogs but about the Larrys of the world whose definition of sustainability is getting through the day. When I visit with Peewee and Larry I am mystified at the parade of "go green" or "save the whales" tee shirts that pass by, studiously ignoring a scruffy dog with a worn out man, apparently intent on insuring a better life for future generations while ignoring a current life that needs help right now. Such is the whimsy of paradox.

Read Charles Handy's book, "*The Age of Paradox*". A great book. It is important to understand and accept paradox as a certainty of a normal existence, otherwise you will go through life flummoxed, and expecting a single logic or certainty will apply to life's issues. As the King of Siam lamented in the musical "*The King and* I", "some things nearly so, some things nearly not – is a puzzlement!" Yes, it is!

Speaking about paradoxes, the religion thing is interesting – seeking truth through assumptions, aka faith. Many need that safety valve. I have been very lucky to have had two excellent Mother-in-Laws, both now gone. Whether you believe in God or not it is an undeniable fact that Alice Reed, my sweet little Mother-in-Law, Joany's Mom, used her unshakable faith as a sustaining rock to hold on to during a terrifying and painful exit. Some people use booze, or drugs, or denial – Alice used God. I wish I could generate her certainty. But isn't it the height of arrogance, and to some degree

cruelty, that strident non-believers would try to remove her source of peace? It's like Larry with his Peewee, believing so much in that dog that sustains him through the days. Easy to tell him it's just a dog, get rid of it and you can eat inside the restaurant.

So on Sundays we sit together, watching, listening, singing. Doing ritual. Each of us in our own way seeking to make the unknown knowable, and at the same time afraid that if the unknown suddenly becomes known it may be something we can't face instead of the answer to our prayers. Uncertainty is difficult to face alone, but with others around us it is easier to accept.

Trying to make the unknown understandable we turn to familiar icons, actions, songs, histories, myths, truths, etc. A sort of philosophical pin the tail on the donkey, but nevertheless comforting, because we are only seeking an answer, not the answer, something believable, not necessarily truth.

"Does God exist" is a great brain teaser, but there are other things to ponder. Like does time exist? Could time exist if there was only space, but no substance? How could you measure the presence, or passage, of time without a substance upon which change can be detected? Time is a measurement of change. Without change, time could not be detected except by our trusty chronometers, but of course they couldn't exist if substance did not exist. Of course neither would we. I need a drink.

Some paradoxes are inconsequential, like why do people put sugar into tea to sweeten, and then add lemon?

Others are weightier, like killing for God's glory. Of course religious folks will tell you those killings occurred because people believed in leaders who did not really have God's ear, (like the Pope I presume – Crusades anyone?) and we are told this by leaders who tell us that they have God's ear. No, I did not serve in the Crusades, but I've read about them.

Yikes, the God conundrum. Does God really exist? Nobody knows, but lots of folks have rock-solid opinions. Believers rely on faith instead of proof, and are scoffed at by those who require proof. Proof is overrated. Supposedly aeronautical engineers can prove that bees are incapable of flight. Nobody can prove that God exists and, paradoxically, nobody can prove God does not exist. I can prove that, if God is a vengeful God, he or she does not exist because I have provided ample reasons for God to strike me dead – and I am still alive.

I am not an agnostic or atheist; I am just an undecided believer in God. My typical wishy-washy position. Spirituality is personal. Religion is institutional. I am a firm believer in religions, up to a point. That point being when a religion runs amok believing it is the only true religion and its members, as God's special chosen people, have an obligation to convert, subjugate, annihilate, etc. to create a worldwide unanimity of God thought. This is the destructive side of religion that is counterpoint to its greater good – providing hope, opportunity, caring and bingo.

Believers through their religions do more good than do non-believers. There are no soup kitchens, clinics, counseling services, shelters or youth programs run by

Atheists. Atheists seem to be self-contained, needing no help and offering none, however they are apparently unable to be secure in their belief, or non-belief. Accordingly, their main activity seems to be denying believers the right to pray, have signs, etc. where Atheist might be exposed to them. Apparently just choosing not to pray isn't good enough – they want to eliminate the sport so nobody else can have fun. The world is full of spoil sports.

It has been said Atheism is a non-prophet organization.

Microorganisms to elephants, primal molds to sequoias – all living plants and animals will kill other living things. However all life forms except man confine killing to issues of self-preservation, and through self-preservation, knowingly or unknowingly, the preservation of one's species.

Man has elevated killing beyond the need for food or self defense to include killing for sport, domination and, most sadly, for beliefs. For family, for country,
for God.

I own a gun. It is in my home and its purpose is to make a big noise to intimidate any robbers that enter the house. Would I use it to kill a robber? If I or my family's life were threatened – yes. Would I kill to keep a possession? No. I would not have killed a person to have gotten any of my possessions. So why should I kill to keep them?

Laguna, 1980.

God and/or the concept of God is like which came first, the chicken or the egg. We are instructed God came first because some human said so, and wrote it down. If God is so powerful why didn't he or she (assuming an anthropomorphic PC deity) write, in their own hand, a proof of their existence, and what we are supposed to do about it? That would have been helpful. Instead all we have to go on is a series of proclamations by a plethora of humans that assure us God exists.

There is no evidence that any living creature except man (and woman) has a concept of God. I believe it is because we the people are the only fauna blessed with the knowledge of our certain death. Ever since that concept caught on thousands of years ago we have been trying to cope, devising desperate counter concepts such as reincarnation, rebirth, heaven/hell, afterlife, and that often referred to state as in "he is in a better place now". We can't seem to be content to just live once. We want an assurance, or a guarantee that when the old peepers close for the last time it ain't over till its over. Ergo religions. Join our club, pay the dues, obey the rules and we can guarantee you an endless ride.

Maybe we invented God instead of God inventing us. Would that make God less important for us? Maybe. We would then face the problem that if we invented God but it turns out there really is no God, then the gig we invented about everlasting life won't happen. But what's so bad about that? Isn't one life enough? Let's not be greedy folks.

We hypothesize, and debate, and analyze in a never-ending search for the meaning of life, seeking an answer for an unanswerable question.

We cannot answer it because life is not the question. Life is the answer. Life is the reason the question can be posed, makes it possible for existence to exist, for without
life to observe the universe, would the universe exist? Perhaps God created life so there would be a vehicle to know existence. Perhaps God did not "create" life – perhaps God is life. Life, the conscious part of the universe.
So we should enjoy and celebrate life – our own plus every other living thing that shares this amazing condition we call existence. Stop questioning and instead accept the answer. God is everywhere, in everything, in each of us, eternal, without beginning or end because without God – life – there is no beginning or end. Beginning and ending are concepts only existing in life.

No God, no existence, no beginning, no end.

There must be universal consciousness, shared by all manifestations of life that we do not individually yet know, or understand. Maybe we vaguely do, and call it God.

Laguna, 1988

Going back to that sustainability thing it seems odd that no religion anticipated the death of our planet by our own hand. There are threats that God could snuff it all out if we aren't good, (now <u>there's</u> vengeance for you!), but not much about a duty to preserve the planet – forever. Why? Probably because up until recently there has been enough stuff to go around, but now we realize we are starting to run out of stuff so preservation paranoia is growing, maybe soon to emerge as a religion near you.

If not a religion it sure will be a huge business.

I am great at questions but short on answers. We all are, because of our inadequate understanding of how the bits and parts of the existence that we think we

When you go to church next Sunday, or whenever, scan the newsletter for unintended inspiration or instruction as evidenced by these excerpts.

"At the evening service the sermon will be "What is hell". Come early and listen to our choir practice."

"Don't let worry kill you – let the church help."

"There will be a meeting in the south and north ends of the church. Children can be baptized at both ends."

"Thursday the Little Mothers Club will meet at 5PM. All wishing to become little mothers please see the minister in his study."

"On Easter Sunday Mrs. Lewis will come forward and lay an egg on the altar."

"The ladies of the church have cast off clothing of every kind and they may be seen in the basement on Friday."

know fit together to form a whole that we don't recognize or understand.

During breakfast this morning at a favorite restaurant I watched an infant boy stretch over his daddy's shoulder to inspect the column supporting a gas lamp. He gripped the pipe so tightly with both tiny hands, his unfocused eyes only inches from its surface. He drooled on it, spoke to it, caressed it, tasted it, and smacked it. He did everything in his power to know this strange object. He finally turned away, satisfied he knew all there was to know about the alien object. After examining with great care, with all his perceptual powers, with all his intellect, he had learned everything he could know about gas lamps, steel columns, natural gas, paint products, etc. By intensive investigation of a single part of the object, he could never comprehend the whole, yet he believed he did.

I know as much about existence – even my own life – as that baby knows about gas lamps. The only difference is that I am aware of my ignorance, and have the social graces not to spit up on myself.

What very clever creatures we are for having only been here for a few seconds of earth's existence. I was forever changed by a T.V. segment by Carl Sagan in which he strolled along a sidewalk a hundred yards long, marking with paint the occurrence of significant events of our orb, such as so many feet to form the earth, so many more till life arrived, etc. He got to the end of the sidewalk and said something like "well what about human history?" and painted the edge at the end of the sidewalk. We are the thickness of a coat of paint on the end of Sagan's 100 yard sidewalk depicting our planet's history!

Apparently we have arrived on earth just in time to save it.

If you have been searching for answers for self improvement, happiness, direction, advice, etc. from the endless sources of authority on such issues, you may want to contemplate the following prayer – author unknown. If you are not in the God camp, change the words "and God gave" to "I was given" to avoid working up a lather over the existence, or not, of God.

> *I asked for Strength...*
> *And God gave me Difficulties*
> *to make me strong.*
> *I asked for Wisdom...*
> *And God gave me Problems to solve.*
> *I asked for Prosperity...*
> *And God gave me Brain and Brawn to*
> *work.*
> *I asked for Courage...*
> *And God gave me Danger to overcome.*
> *I asked for Love...*
> *And God gave me troubled people to*
> *help.*
> *I asked for Favors...*
> *And God gave me Opportunities.*
> *I received nothing I wanted...*
> *I received everything I needed.*

# Section Six

Of course architects intend to play a vital role in the planet's rescue. As mentioned earlier (I think) the process of building man made environments is a very messy business, consuming and polluting at alarming rates. It is now de rigueur for architects to obtain LEED certification, Leadership in Energy and Environmental Design, one of several organizations that have sprung up to "inform", in academia speak, the architectural and engineering professions in the utilization of non-polluting renewable resources and energy production. If you closely inspect the concepts of renewability they are similar to a perpetual motion machine.

The climate issue has become so strong an influence on architecture that many offices now have more LEED certificates hanging than architectural registrations. A little priority shift. But tracking the changing directions that architecture takes is a constant adventure. During my short span I have seen architects jump from ship to ship– Corbu/Wright/Mies/Enzo/Gehry/etc./etc., each in their time a design messiah whose flocks defended and promoted the new order with single minded zeal. Out with the old, in with the new. Apparently in their opinion little design value was accomplished prior to the emergence of the latest and greatest.

My own experiences as an apprentice dragged me through several of these new "paradigms" (I swore I would not use that word) of design. My first mentor was Frank Lloyd Wright, 1953. Not a bad start. However as discussed earlier some disturbing signs emerged, such as simultaneous construction of the *Boomer* and *Adleman* residences side by side in the Arizona desert. Both were originally designed for different sites in different states, but instead were adapted to a new location. Which is o.k. Happens all the time. Called "site adaptability". But why two totally different design philosophies – **Usonian Automatic**, a cast concrete block panel system based on a rigid rectangular grid, next to a **Desert Organic**, a system of desert stone exposed in cast concrete based on a rigid triangular grid?

As you know I was fresh from High School at the time. Science has recently discovered what parents have known for eons – the part of the brain concerned with making decisions is not fully formed until our early twenties. So my unfinished brain did not understand the proof of Mr. Wright's genius that surrounded me as I worked. I will still critically challenge using plans designed for a specific site being transported to alien conditions. Yes, Phoenix in July is an alien condition. The consistent logic that unified the startling difference in design discipline and aesthetic between the two constructions was the clue I missed.

Mr. Wright, unlike many other icons, was comfortable evolving a new design without abandoning an old one. His designs were always ordered by a consistent grid for layout, but he varied even that core design element, using a square, rectangular, triangular or circular grid with equal success. He also was at ease working with wood, stone, concrete – even canvas. Unfortunately he left us before titanium became "economically" (ha ha) available.

During my intermittent exposures to design at Arizona State University I labored in a transition from Mr. Wright's philosophies to the then hot architectural design popular in academic circles known as "the International Style". If you are fortunate to visit NYC compare the United Nations Building, an icon of the international style, to Wright's organic solution at the Guggenheim Museum, and you will see the opposing forces that were at work on my semi-formed mind.

The International Style abhorred any form of ornamentation. Only absolutely functional things were allowed on the skin of a building. The United Nation's Building is an example of what that looks like. If it is true that less is more, why aren't rainbows a single color? It is hard to believe that the same profession that created St. Paul's Cathedral also produced the United Nation's building.

Well, the current hot young architects evidently will have none of this less is more stuff. New buildings now sprout startling amounts of expensive scrap metal bolted all over them. Awnings, poles, screens, "statements", "accents", false windows, etc. are crawling all over the buildings. Don't worry. It is another fad that will fade. Soon I hope.

As noted earlier it has been famously proclaimed that "Architects are the pattern givers for society". A bit grand. And I hope incorrect because I don't want the sorry state of society blamed on me.

Another statement often heard is the analogy that an architect is like an orchestra conductor, directing various specialties in the creation of a complete piece. Not so. The analogy is perhaps – if there is one – that the architect is the composer, writing all the parts, and the conductor is the contractor, directing the assembly of all the parts and the owner owns the music hall. Well, whatever architects are or are not it bothers me that my profession spawns so many messiahs that evidently believe architecture is the end all of art, and architects are "it", and by the use of photography and public relations agents they can impose their latest idea of design on the world.

It is always good to remember that you will soon just be someone's ancestor.

My hospital stay at A.I. DuPont allowed me to observe the complexity of healthcare in operation, (no pun intended) 24/7, over a prolonged time. The latent architect in me took note of everything from how many holes were in each acoustical ceiling tile to the duration, interaction, and change cycle of various staff shifts. I learned that everything in my limited world had a positive or negative effect on me. Food cart good. Phlebotomist cart bad. Sunny window good. Nighttime – all bad. I was learning at the time, but was unaware, of the power of psychoneuroimmunology, PNI; the branch of neuroscience that investigates the impact environment has on our immune systems. My prolonged exposure to an acute care environment planted seeds that would later sprout as a healthcare facilities architect.

In 2007 Devenney Group was honored to be included in the underwriting of a remarkable book entitled "*The Fourth Factor", A Historical Perspective on Architecture and Medicine",* edited by John Michael Currie, A.I.A., FRSH which details the history of architecture for healing beginning in ancient Egypt. Circa 400 B.C. Hippocrates wrote "The art consists in three factors – the disease, the patient, and the physician." The book adds a fourth factor – place – acknowledging that architecture and environment also play a part in the healing process.

Only very recently have we begun to understand how very profound is the role the fourth factor plays in healing.

The marriage of architecture and neuroscience was conceived and organized by John Eberhard, FAIA, who hosted a workshop in 2002 for architects and neuroscientists to explore connections between the brain and the environment, specifically architecturally produced environments. The attendees formed the nucleus of an organization which will provide fundamental changes in architectural design, especially in healthcare facilities – The Academy of Neuroscience for Architecture, ANA.

Another group is investigating Evidence Based Design, EBD, promoted by the Center for Health Design. EBD is off to a shaky start, promoting collective anecdotal reports and single experiments as proof, or "evidence". Evidence means if you do X then Y <u>might</u> happen. Proof says if you do X, then Y <u>will</u> happen. Without proof that a design decision will produce a positive result for sustainability or environmental goals – or more importantly for medical outcomes - selling such design to cash strapped clients is tough.

Stress is the arch enemy of our immune system, our internal chemistry set that directs the healing process. Healthcare facility architects should paraphrase the physician's oath – "First eliminate environmental stress". Accordingly it would be nice to have <u>proof</u> rather than "evidence" that if I decide to employ specific design elements or solutions that those decisions would actually help to reduce stress.

One of the most seriously botched design elements in hospitals is, of all places, the patient room. Jain Malkin, A.I.A., one of the most respected and innovative designers of healthcare spaces, pointedly observed to me that "the basic design of a patient room has not changed significantly since 1900, with the exception of occupant load". Moving from four bed wards to private rooms was a good start, but we can't stop there.

Responding to Jain's challenge health care design professionals have increasingly emphasized "patient centered care", designing towards a "patient focus". Unfortunately much of this effort is focused where the patients are not – 5-star lobbies, healing gardens, upscale shopping, fine dining, and MRIs that resemble a day at the beach.

We hope these efforts contribute towards the goal of providing a good experience for the patient, but often overlooked is the fact that a patient's satisfaction with his or her "experience" is based much more on quality care and good outcomes rather than on décor and amenities.

"Patient focused" design abounds throughout hospitals, but is least employed where it is needed most – the area of the hospital that has the most environmental and experiential influence on the patient's neurological, psychological, intellectual and biological systems – The Patient's Room, (possessive).

Recent statistics indicate most positive satisfaction scores derive from experiences occurring within the patient's room, and most of the patient's stay is spent in his or her room. Virtually 100% of patient/visitor interaction occurs in the patient's room. Almost all caregiver/patient conferencing is held in the patient's room. Mobil everything is being brought to the patient's room to avoid moving the patient. There is a rapid increase in utilization of the patient room as the site for interventional care. Family/friends are increasingly urged to participate in care giving – in the patient's room. Patient rooms are increasingly expected to accommodate multiple acuity uses.

Considering the above, why do patient rooms continue to look like their original 1900 models, apparently designed primarily as storage for patient observation, recovery, and earliest possible discharge? Why do they continue to be ridiculously small, incapable of adequately fulfilling their ever expanding role(s)?

It is partially because that unlike other areas of the hospital such as surgery or imaging, there is no "user group" at the design table lobbying for space in the patient room. The patient is not present and so the patient room relies on nursing staff for representation. Unfortunately nursing's considerable knowledge and creativeness seems to be lower in the pecking order for space allocations than "major" departments, such as administration, or dietary.

Few creative solutions exist – if any – that will allow a constantly increasing number of functions to successfully occur in a space that never grows in size. Maybe, we should size the room to accommodate its functions instead of stuffing as many activities as possible into a "standard" patient room.

There is a persistent myth that size and cost are directly proportional, resulting in the assumption that if the hospital's average cost per square foot is $300 – (good luck!) – then adding 50 square feet to a patient room will cost $15,000. Not so, because all that's added is 50 square feet of floor and ceiling plus 400 cubic feet of air – with no additional expense for doors, light fixtures, headwall connections, windows, medical equipment, IT, plumbing fixtures, etc. – in short, cheap space..

Another reason patient rooms are targets for space squeezing is because of the multiplier factor – 200 rooms times 50 s.f. each equals 10,000 added square feet. For the average 200-bed hospital this equates to approximately a 4% increase in overall size which erroneously and unfortunately will be viewed as a 4% increase in the overall hospital cost.

Also contributing to patient rooms being shorted for space is an unfortunate slogan in the industry, "put our money where we make money", specifically clinical spaces, apparently under the mistaken belief that money comes from the surgery room. No, it doesn't – it comes from the patient's payer. There seems to be a beginning of an understanding of this linkage to money evident in the current zeal for creating good patient satisfactions and experiences which supposedly will encourage patients to return, bringing their payer's money with them. So shouldn't we pamper the payer by pampering the patient, to get good patient satisfaction scores?

In addition to giving attention to the size of the room we should also recognize the <u>owner</u> of the room – <u>the patient</u>. The patient is a guest in the hospital's hotel and, just like at Marriott, the guest should "own" their room. It is the patient's space, a temporary but critically comforting ownership, a space that must serve with equal grace family gatherings as well as critical medical procedures. To accomplish this the patient's room must accommodate multiple activity zones:

1. A family/visitor zone for patient socialization and support.

2. A patient zone for patient privacy and control.

3. A staff zone for caregiver activities and equipment.

Successfully integrating all three is one of the most challenging hospital design problems.

Organizations such as The Center for Health and the Institute of Medicine have developed specific design criteria to help optimize patient safety, wellbeing, healing rate and outcome quality, while reducing length of stay. Successful implementation of these initiatives coupled with the need to accommodate increasing functional requirements will drive the size of the patient's room larger and yes, marginally more expensive.

Isn't it logical that an adequately sized and equipped room could more than offset its increased cost by reducing errors, reducing length of stays, reducing patient movements, increasing staff efficiency and satisfaction, etc. plus increased patient satisfaction and outcome quality?

Unfortunately when I advance the idea of making patient rooms larger than the 1900 model in meetings with hospital CFOs, contractors and "program managers" I feel about as welcome as a pedophile at a PTA meeting.

Through the work of pioneering neuroscientists engaging with architects much is being learned about the enormous impact the hospital building, and especially the patient's room, has on the patient's healing opportunities. It is as important as medical technologies, therapies, surgeries or pharmacology.

Few projects offer more demanding architectural challenges than hospital facilities.

They are challenging because of the complex integration of technologies, clinical pathways, medical specialties and the vast array of administrative, regulatory and reimbursement criteria that govern every activity within a hospital. But even more important than these challenges is the sole reason for the project to exist – **the patient**. <u>The degree to which the challenges of a single patient are met determines the relative success of the entire project.</u>

Don't hang up! This is not another yap about patient centered care issues. We all know the efficacy of snacks on demand, a window with a view, or gowns that have no butt gap.

Assuming good safety and quality care will provide for the patient's physical wellbeing, what is our further responsibility as designers? The patient's sensory wellbeing – not to be confused <u>with the patient's sense of wellbeing.</u> The patient's sense of wellbeing can impact his/her satisfaction

scores, but the patient's <u>sensory wellbeing</u> will dramatically impact his/her healing process.

A sense of wellbeing is predominately a conscious evaluation of ones surroundings, which can be positively therapeutic if stress levels are positively controlled.

Sensory wellbeing is most often informed by our subconscious state responding to uncontrollable autonomic responses to one's environment.

The wellbeing of our sensory state plays a vital role in achieving homeostasis in the vastly complex organism we call our body. In summary, everything external to our body has a direct influence within our body.

Richard Farson, PhD., through his speaking, writing and advocacy via groups such as the Design Intelligence Institute has worked for years to bring collaboration between the neurosciences and environmental design. Esther Sternberg, MD in her recent book *"Healing Spaces"* presents a comprehensive study of the direct link between our surroundings and our immune system.

It is fitting that scientists – e.g. physicians, and neuroscientists – rather than designers are leading the way to scientifically construct design solutions based on <u>proofs</u>. The architectural profession via The A.I.A. Academy of Architecture for Health and The American College of Healthcare Architects should lend support to their endeavors, participating in academically controlled investigations rather than assuming a volume of anecdotal observations constitutes a proof.

After centuries of intuitively designing volumes, surfaces and spaces that invoke respect, or peace, or reverence architects are beginning to try to understand why what they do actually works – most times. Architects such as Juhani Pallasmaa in his book, *"The Eyes of the Skin"*, have begun to awaken the understanding of designers regarding the power of the unintended consequences of their work.

Through the work of pioneering neuroscientists engaging with architects much is being learned about the enormous impact the hospital building, and especially the patient's room, has on the patient's healing opportunities. It is as important as medical technologies, therapies, surgeries or pharmacology.

Assembling a comprehensive understanding of the impact of a room design will have on the immune system is not possible by studying the room as a unit. Each element of the room must be independently evaluated and then the synergism of their combination analyzed to enable a true understanding of how the room will impact a patient's immune system.

Webster: "Synergism" – the interaction of conditions such that the total effect is greater than the sum of individual parts." How to effectively manage such knowledge requires a universal agreement of definitions and measurements.

Devenney: "Design" – The process of creating an aesthetic and/or functional addition or change to the natural environment.

<u>Devenney</u>: "Design Element" – Any element of the natural environment that can be altered or controlled by human intervention.

Stress from any source can compromise a patient's immune system, which is so vital for healing to occur. Accordingly, avoiding or reducing stress in the hospital environment can have a significant positive impact on healing. By example the simple act of admission to the hospital can induce stress. Comparisons have been drawn between admission to a hospital and induction to a jail:

- They take away your clothes and valuables.

- You are closely monitored at all times.

- Your choices are limited.

- You are assigned a room and a number.

- You are not allowed to leave.

- You are given limited control over your environment.

Entering into an environment of uncertainty and anxiety is a very stressful experience.

Simple things mean a lot. For instance having your clothes replaced with a gown that shows your naked butt every time you move can jump start your stress level unless you are very confident with your body or are an exhibitionist. Every source of stress can have a powerfully destructive effect on your immune system – the healing system.

Unfortunately the naked butt syndrome is only the beginning of your stay in stressor land. Neuroscientists are methodically converting "evidence" to more usable and saleable "proof" that specific design decisions will enhance medical outcomes. Each element of the patient's environment that contributes to stress is now being identified, quantified for severity, and suggested mitigations developed.

Neuroscience will do for healthcare buildings what Mr. Otis did for multistory buildings – enable a new dimension of building functions. Now the physician's oath of "first do no harm" can truly be adapted for hospital architects – "first provide no stressors". Buildings will someday soon be an environment that is an integral part of the healing process, not just a space in which it occurs.

Having a piano in the lobby is very nice, but difficult to see or hear from Room 312. A Healing Garden is wonderful, for those who can get to it. Maybe it's time – way past time – that we truly focus our design efforts (and a reasonable budget) on the patient (singular) and the patient's (possessive) room.

Hospitals are expensive to build, so many designers have been exploring how to segregate functions that do not need to be inside the hospital and instead provide them in a separate, sometimes connected, less costly building.

It is easy to separate the space program, (a list of all spaces required for the design with data regarding dimensions, functions, occupants, etc.) for a typical hospital into two groups of spaces, those that must meet "I", institutional, occupancy requirements, and those that can occupy less restrictive "B" business occupancy construction.

There are dramatic variances between "B" and "I" facilities in cost for initial construction, annual utilities, and annual maintenance. "B" functions can be built for 50% less than "I" functions. Also, "B" functions consume 50% less power to operate than the 24/7/365 "I" functions.

There are also significant differences in design and construction schedules, primarily due to different requirements for permitting and licensure. This is especially true in California because of complex and costly construction codes applicable to hospital "I" occupancy that requires extensive state review, while permit review time for "B" occupancy is comparatively insignificant. Time is money.

Simplistically, the two occupancy ratings could be located in two separate buildings, however in reality for functional reasons there must be a close adjacency for easy access between all areas of a hospital. Accordingly, the scenario of two separate buildings does not provide a satisfactory solution in many cases.

However, some hospital functions can indeed be housed outside the hospital, and even away from the campus. By example, purely business functions such as accounting or Human Resources can easily be remotely located. Even some clinical functions such as radiology reading have moved out of the hospital, and even out of the country! This trend will accelerate, as the hospital as we now know it increasingly becomes a provider of outpatient services in an outpatient facility rather than within the hospital. This is another reason to begin separating "I" and "B" occupancies – doing so will provide facility flexibility to accommodate the change in healthcare processes that are occurring ever more rapidly.

If not separated in two separate buildings, what are other options? A single building can be divided into an "I" occupancy section, and a "B" occupancy section. This can be achieved by a vertical separation between wings of a structure, or by horizontal separation by dedicating floors to "B" or "I" occupancy.

The most successful scenario appears to be a horizontal stratification, with the ground level containing all diagnostic, treatment and support services. Each function, being at ground level, can expand horizontally without disruption to any other function. Special patient care units (ICU, CCU) are also on this level, with general patient medical/surgical and birthing functions located on floors over the special care units, thus all nursing care is in a single dedicated tower.

Section Seven

Lessening stress in the hospital unfortunately has a limited value for healing because of time. Too little of it. Since 1983 the Feds have reimbursed hospitals (a percentage of their costs) for all medical procedures based on DRGs – Diagnosis Related Groups.

DRGs pay a fixed amount for each procedure, regardless of how much time or cost a hospital invests. A knee replacement is worth $XX – every time, everywhere, every patient. This is why patients are discharged almost before coming out of anesthetic – the sooner the hospital gets you out of the hospital the more of the meager DRG reimbursement is left unspent. Unfortunately rushing discharges can contribute to a higher percentage of readmits – a costly error.

Psycho Nuero Immunology (PNI) will become even more effective as the primary location of healthcare delivery shifts from an acute care hospital to a continuing care center to the patient's home – a journey to an ever less stressful environment. Only the most dedicated hypochondriac would prefer a stay in the hospital to staying at home.

So what does DRGs have to do with PNI? For psychoneuroimmunology to be optimally effective the patient needs to be immersed in a stress free environment during her or his healing process. So PNI can provide significant value to patients having conditions requiring long term stay, but less value to the two-day itinerant patient.

This is a bummer for patient healing, but PNI has other values. Some stressors are personalized and episodic, specific to the patient experience, others are "pandemic" global stressors that impact everyone within the environment – like the caregiver staff. Stress not only affects our immune systems, it also affects our mental systems resulting in exhaustion, anxiety, loss of focus, and reduced mental acuity. Just the sort of condition you do not want your caregiver working in while mixing your chemo dosage. So in addition to healing the patients by directly impacting the their immune systems, PNI also contributes to caregiver wellbeing, resulting in fewer errors, supporting hospital goals for a "safe environment" that depends largely on a stress free environment.

Over 75% of healthcare spending is for ongoing treatment of chronic diseases which sporadically may require a stay in a hospital, but less expensive and more effective care can be provided via supervised home care.

Completely equipped and staffed mobile medical clinics providing scheduled visits to the patient's home plus a host of medical remote monitoring technologies will make a continuous and efficient home care system possible.

Studies have demonstrated that well-designed patient environments contribute to faster recovery and better outcomes. This remarkable correlation no doubt depends a great deal on the fact that the enhanced environment influences caregivers, as well as patients. If we acknowledge that environment has a positive or negative influence on individuals, it probably follows that the degree to which one is influenced is directly proportional to length of time spent in the environment, which highlights my point: Patients come and go, but caregivers remain forever.

Certainly aesthetics help, but a good looking building and interior design is only the veneer of the hospital experience. Peel away the aesthetics and we find stress is generated by virtually every source – sometimes even the aesthetics. Background noises, air temperature,

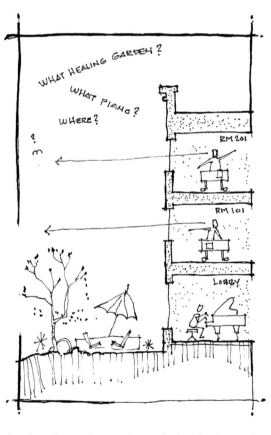

light sources, light levels, orientation of the bed to the door and/or window, caregiver activity levels, etc. all contribute to stress – and can be controlled to some degree by good planning and design. Shape up architects.

Much ado (what is "ado"?) is made about having a room with a pleasant view, probably difficult to obtain in some neighborhoods. Also, if your point of view is lying in bed ten feet from the window, your view is compromised, because if you are on an upper floor your view will be only sky since you can't look down. More important than the view is that a window is a reassurance of a way out, that outside is still there, knowing the weather and time of day, etc. It is not the only important view. Of course the view to the T.V. is important for what is called a "positive distraction", like you won't notice the nurse entering with a big honker needle. Other views are important. The bathroom. The corridor. Visitor seating. The ceiling.

Views of the piano in the lobby or the fountain in the healing garden from the patient's bed are limited. However with the magic of technology, a network of surveillance cameras controlled by the patient via the T.V. could bring lots of "positive distraction" by allowing the patient to visually participate, in real time, in activities in the parking lot, the healing garden, in the lobby, the cafeteria, the chapel, the CEO's office – ha, ha.

Of course there are privacy protection issues to consider. In a society where you are under surveillance grocery shopping, in the parking lot, on the streets, locatable 24/7 via your cell phone, and your private life can be investigated by any competent teenager with a computer – what privacy are we trying to protect? Wake up folks – your on candid camera, and computer.

You may have guessed I am no Nobel Prize candidate for PNI understanding, but it is important to share with you PNI as I understand it. Since most of you are not neuroscientists, my dumbed down translation via my dumb brain may hopefully result in something understandable.

There are two environments that impact our neurologic and immune systems – the <u>actual</u> environment existing outside our bodies, and a <u>perceived</u> environment that exists within us. It is the latter that enables placebo and nocebo effects. The actual environment and the powerful forces it controls within us are difficult to impact via architecture, but possible. This is the biggest challenge and opportunity for the design of facilities for patient care.

Evidently stress can be somewhat controlled by "positive distractions". Hypnosis is a powerful tool routinely used to allow patients to ignore stress. Also interesting is the strange science of placebos and nocebos and their effect on our brain's perceptions and its subsequent directions to the chemistry set of our bodies. It has been demonstrated during clinical trials for new pharmaceuticals that in a surprising percentage of patients the placebo is as effective as the real thing. I've always been told it's not nice, or even dangerous, to fool Mother Nature. Maybe not always. If you tell a patient a fake pill will reduce pain and his brain believes it, and turns off some of the pain switches, what's the harm? Viva placebo!

103

The key is <u>telling</u> the patient the pill <u>will</u> work. The <u>pill</u> does not trigger the brain, the <u>instruction</u> does. So placebo is mostly hypnosis, or in big words, cognitive behavior therapy. Nocebo is the placebo's evil twin. If you tell someone you have put a drug in his food that will make him sick, he will very often get sick. Nocebos are what makes voodoo magic work.

I have obtained verifiable and dramatic proof that nocebos do work. While I was a puppy draftsman I worked with a classic hypochondriac who was so impressionable we could make him sick and go home just by constantly asking questions like "have you heard about the new flu virus", or offering fake observations like "you look a little flushed this morning". We would start an office pool to see who was closest to the time he left for home. My little experiment to test his squeamish level was to take his coffee mug (always covered by a hanky to keep out stray virus) and replace his coffee with red drafting ink and a few smoked oysters from my snack stash (I know – weird). There is a medical phrase – projectile vomiting – which was instantly demonstrated when he took the hanky off the mug. Barfed like a fire hose – and left for home. My boss was unamused, nor interested in the lessons science could learn from my experiment. I got to clean the room while the rest of the grossed out staff got to take a break.

Circling back to the issue at hand – creating a stress free environment to enhance healing – placebo and nocebo instruction can be physically incorporated in the design of the environment. Placebo sound; waterfall. Nocebo sound; beeping alarms. Placebo view; trees.

Nocebo view; dumpster. To be effective the placebo/nocebo effect needs instruction – "the tree is pretty and it <u>will</u> help you heal". So architecture must assist the patient to provide their own instructions such as making the window a prominent feature of the room, or reinforcing the waterfall sound with artwork of water features. Other prompts such as a view of the bathroom may not be as uplifting to the spirit, but is equally important to the healing process. For post surgical patients it is important that the bowels and urinary tract begin full operation as soon as possible. Studies have shown a view of the toilet will stimulate thoughts of you know what. So yes, the view of the porcelain may well contribute more than a tree (unless you are a dog) to waking up our vital functions from their personal battle with anesthesia. I have seen some artwork that could also be helpful, but it may be too graphic for those with a limited sense of humor.

Speaking of art as a physical stimulus, what's with the ad for Cialis, the sexual average raiser that shows a man and a woman in separate bathtubs, usually in the middle of nowhere, reaching across and touching fingers? They don't even look at each other. Shouldn't the ad promote togetherness? I'm just asking.

Follow along while I leap back to the design of hospitals. You know by now my bias for considering the patient's room as the most important space for healing. Other areas of the hospital provide intervention or diagnosis, but the patient's ability to recover from that work occurs in the patient's room. I made much about the patient's private space, but there are pros and cons to "private" rooms. They are not always the best solution. Having a cellmate has its benefits. My own experience (quite good) was as a member of a 20-bed ward. Semiprivate has benefits. Socialization can be a major "positive distraction" eliminating a sense of isolation, meeting your cell mates' visitors (especially if you have none of your own), eaves dropping on doctor/patient consultations, sharing edible gifts, listening to phone conversations, etc. can be entertaining, and a distraction from pain and anxiety.

But private rooms allow more flexibility in running the hotel portion of the hospital. No problems associated with mixing infectious patients, male/female matches (possibly a source of positive distraction?), geriatric/pediatric pairings, not to mention mixing visiting families. The hospital's answer to the philosophical question "can't we all just get along" is – no. There are creative floor plan solutions that can accommodate two patients in the same room while still providing some privacy for each. Unfortunately those solutions involve increased square footage, the mythical driver of cost so dear to the bean counters, and also sometimes increased walking for nurses, which is not a myth and is truly bad.

Although much design attention is rightfully focused on patients, the primary design should focus on the staff, especially the direct caregivers. Lots of design time is devoted to the patient's experience so they will come back – a weird idea. But most attention should focus on those who treat the patients – caregivers.

WHICH WAY TO THE HEALING GARDEN?

You might have had the experience of going to a beautiful restaurant serving excellent food and having terrible service. What did you tell your friends about the restaurant? Excellent healthcare can be provided in the most depressing surroundings – and the patient will remember the excellent care. When poor care is delivered in a beautiful surrounding, the patient will remember the poor care.

The moral of all this is that *service counts more than surroundings*. A beautiful setting cannot overcome a surly or incompetent staff; but a cheerful, capable caregiver can overcome a lack of facility ambience. A well-designed facility cannot provide an excellent experience or a lasting relationship. It can only supply a tool to be used by caregivers to accomplish those goals.

It just may be that the environment's role is as important – perhaps even *more* important – in providing support for caregivers as for patients. The reason is simple: It is easier to provide quality care in a well-designed facility.

You've probably guessed where this is going. It is at least as important to create excellent environments in the "back rooms of the house" as it is in the "parlor". Doing so promotes staff pride and enthusiasm, and can be an effective retention and recruitment tool.

Architects can create an environment, but people make it work. It is obvious that concern for the patient flows from caregivers, not from the wallpaper. Perhaps architecture's greatest contribution to patient well-being is to create environments that support staff and family - the caregivers. Accordingly major design goals should enhance caregivers' working environments to reduce stress, promote communication, provide respite, reinforce spirituality, save time and (in answer to a universal request) provide adequately sized, usably designed, and appropriately located storage.

Much has been written about a "front room/back room" or "on-stage/backstage" design philosophy which by definition divides the focus of healthcare facility design into two categories. Certainly there are vast differences in functional design requirements between the main lobby and a nurses' lounge – but should there be a difference between them in the environmental ambience expressed, or the effort expended to achieve it, or the quality of the experience generated by the room? Is it more important to impress our guests than to respect our family?

It is interesting to note that our living rooms are usually the showcase of our homes, while we actually live in the family room, or the kitchen, or the den. Although we entertain our guests in the living room, we actually live in another, more comfortable part of the house. We're seeking comfort. Where is finding comfort more important, and so difficult to find, than in a hospital?

In order to design for comfort, it is instructive to analyze what can disrupt comfort. Some design elements that can significantly reduce the comfort level of any surrounding include:

- Persistent, aggravating sounds

- Shiny surfaces

- Poorly controlled lighting

- No view of the exit

- No view of the outside

- Sterile or institutional furnishings

- Seeing strangers who can presumably also see you

- Accent colors, if they are not your colors

- Temperature excess (either way)

- Odd smells

- Lack of Privacy

- Etc., etc.

Knowing the importance of comfort, why do we find so many hospital environments to be so disquieting? There are several reasons – none of them valid. In sum, issues of infection control, security, regulatory compliance, and presumed space efficiency (thought wrongly to be equivalent to cost efficiency) tend to lead designers to create fairly Spartan environments. Also, many architects who are drawn to hospital design are attracted to it for that very reason: a chance, in their view, to exercise a Spartan design philosophy, sometimes summarized as "less is more". (In fact, it isn't). Another chilling architectural mantra describes buildings as "machines for living," which may have a certain interest for high-tech hospital design, but it is a rather depressing analogy for one seeking an environment offering comfort, solace, and hope.

There are moments of clarity when I realize I could have specialized in something easier, like hotels or schools, but the challenge of healthcare still floats my boat. Hey there school and hotel architects, before you send me nasty letters remember our earlier conversation about the complexity of hospital design, boasting we are number two in regulatory complexity – right behind nuclear energy. As the Irish farmers boast – "strong like a bull, smart like a tractor".

SOME ARCHITECTS SEEM TO HAVE A
SPATIAL AWARENESS DEFICIENTCY

WHERE DO TAHITIANS GO TO RELAX?

Section Eight

Hospitals have enormous potential to be so much more than hospitals. They can be a vital community center. The following is a pep talk I gave to a hospital client. I thought it was quite good but the audience didn't quite grasp the point. Maybe you will – I hope.

> Why not sell healthcare like Detroit sells cars? Granted, healthcare is (supposed to be) a service, and a car is a product. However, there is much instruction we can take from the car business that can greatly improve our healthcare business.

> Note: When addressing a hospital it is politically wise to refer to healthcare as a service instead of the commodity that it is.

> For the car business, selling you the car is not their major objective. Purchasing the car is a single event. The car business sees that event not as the close of a sale, but the opening of an opportunity to establish a long-term relationship. They seek not only to make the sale good for them and good for you (a "good experience"), but also to make you an integral part of their culture. Does your hospital inspire your customers to buy and use hats, bumper stickers, shirts, beer mugs, posters, key chains, etc. with your logo on them?

How often have you heard people say "I'm a Ford man and my whole family are Ford people", or "My Daddy was a Ford man and so am I". How often have you heard "I'm a Woopy General Hospital man and durn proud of it"? Do you inspire loyalty?

Maybe Detroit isn't selling cars, maybe not a product. Granted they make "the experience" of buying a car as enjoyable as possible, but are they really just selling <u>A</u> car, <u>A</u> product <u>AN</u> experience? No, they are selling <u>a continuing relationship</u>.

➤   They finance for you

➤   They provide service after the sale

➤   They establish specific follow-up care

➤   They provide "added value" such as roadside service

➤   They remember your name

➤   They send you a Birthday card

➤   They imprint their brand on your forehead – and you like it.

The "car" becomes the "Cadillac". It is not a car, it is a brand. If you buy a Cadillac, Cadillac wants to be certain you will never buy any other brand of car for the rest of your life – and that your family and friends will share your loyalty to Cadillac.

Why should we not apply car business techniques to our healthcare business? Let's assume we agree to define healthcare as a *business* that provides a *service*, and without a successful business there can be no service.

Each patient encounter should not be limited to an episodic event, a *sale*, but instead be considered an opportunity for your institution to form a lasting relationship with the patient and the patient's family and friends. If my car dealership can send me a Birthday card, or a free car wash, why not my medical caregivers? Who is thinking about me? It is now in vogue for hospitals to provide patients with a "special experience", taking cues from the entertainment, restaurant and spa industries. These industries recognize that if their customers have a good experience they will voluntarily come back for more entertainment, dining or relaxation. Do we really believe if a patient has a "special experience" having a colonoscopy they will seek their first opportunity to return for another experience? Of course not. We may electively return to Disneyland, or a fine restaurant, for another experience –but will we electively return to the hospital for another "special experience"? Hardly. There is virtually **NO** medical experience that is enjoyable.

So is the point of providing patient service as a "special experience" solely to make the stay as enjoyable as possible, or to promote faster healing, or better outcomes? Certainly these reasons are important, but do you want your relationship with the patient to stop when they leave? What could possible bring them back short of a relapse, or an injury or illness?

The reason Women's Centers, or Birthing Center, or Birthplaces – whatever hot current name is attached to the old O.B. Department – have been receiving great attention for design stems from a belief that if a woman gives birth to her child in your hospital and has a "good experience", she will forever be bonded to your institution for future medical care not only for herself, but also her family.

Think about it. If in the future this woman's husband needs a heart transplant, will she bring him in based on her really great experience in your O.B. Department? What about the insurance carrier or the Cardiologist's say in the matter?

But she might if instead of having just a special experience she more importantly had formed a special relationship with your institution, a relationship that continued over the years, forming a bond of trust, caring and loyalty. A special experience – extended. A relationship that made her constantly aware that in addition to a great O.B. experience, your hospital also provides heart transplants and many other services – medical and non-medical – to make her entire life experience more secure, productive and positive.

For many years our firm has been entirely specialized in healthcare design, watching our clients grapple with various procedures and processes that supposedly would define their institution as a special place, offering special services – TQM, the birthing experience, the Disney way, be a service not a commodity, wellness promotion, patient centered care, the Planetree experience, community outreach programs, the healing experience, etc. etc.

All of these programs strive to enhance the episodic experience one has during diagnostic or treatment procedures. A good thing to do. Increasing service quality, producing better outcomes, generating happier customers/patients/guests are all critically necessary endeavors. But aren't they goals that every hospital should strive for? Shouldn't these values be the norm instead of the exception? Shouldn't the public expect such service? Thus as you meet your goals, the public gets what it expects. Does this thrill the public? No. You either deliver their expectations, or fail. Neither option will cause individuals to buy your tee shirts, and forever more sing your song.

What could change this "no win" situation in which we find ourselves? We can try to exceed their expectations by <u>doing the same things only better</u>. Indeed "exceeding expectations" is the latest mantra being preached to every business. But if we consistently exceed expectations, exceeded expectations become "normal expectations". We must constantly raise the bar. How high can we jump? There must be a limit, then we're stuck.

How about meeting the public's expectations in a holistic way that far exceeds a narrow focus on the episodic event of treatment. Let's provide them with a value they <u>did not expect</u> – a lasting caring relationship about each individual, and his or her family and community.
Developing ways to promote and sustain such relationships will require a commitment of your organization and its policies and procedures. It may also alter your mission and vision statements. It will dramatically alter your strategic planning.

So where does design enter the equation? How can relationships be fostered through design? Your buildings, landscape, furniture, printed materials, food, uniforms, signage – the entire environment of your institution – establishes your statement of who you are, what you do, and how you do it. Your built environment involves all of our sensory systems in a very powerful way. Accordingly, your environment is the key vehicle that will enable lasting relationships to be formed – or not. By example, consider that HIPAA can be a powerful positive tool instead of the latest federal curse. Why not promote and accentuate, by design, the fact that you are striving to protect a person's most personal asset – their privacy – instead of complaining about the @#!! new red tape.

Some of the facility developments that can form a critical mass of services that will make your facility a positive and indispensable community force are:

1. A separate area dedicated to post partum services such as depression counseling, infant medical care, infant safety, breast-feeding.
2. A freestanding clinic for continuing pediatric and adolescent medical and wellness care.
3. A daycare for well children available for hospital employees as well as patient visitors.
4. A daycare for sick children observation.
5. A daycare for the elderly, a respite for family caregivers.
6. A visitor room and yard for pet visitations.
7. An assembly room with clinical space for community health screenings, school physicals, etc.
8. Classrooms for home economics, healthy cooking.
9. An expanded physical therapy department to allow provision for weight loss, cardiovascular conditioning and

other prescribed and supervised exercise programs for the public.

10. An industrial medical program for executive health, workman's compensation rehabilitation, ergonometrics, and work hardening programs etc.

11. A full service ophthalmology clinic and optician services.

12. A full service audiology center.

13. A full service business center available to patients, visitors, and medical staff.

14. A concierge alcove in the Lobby dispensing information and refreshments.

15. Provide courtesy parking – no tipping allowed.

16. A full service dental clinic.

17. A complete education and conference facility with a media studio/workroom.

18. An interior/exterior playground for visiting children.

19. A video arcade for adolescent visitors, and staff who have adolescent tendencies.

20. A retail book store.

21. A retail health nutritional store

22. A commercial hotel.

23. A retail florist shop.

24. A retail pharmacy.

25. A retail Durable Medical Equipment shop.

26. Office space for insurance providers.

27. Office space for financial and legal consultants.

28. Spaces for religious ministrations.

29. A comprehensive alternative medicine center.
30. An allergy clinic.
31. A pain management clinic
32. Sports medicine – with sports. Sponsor/direct amateur athletics in various sports, i.e. soccer leagues, tennis tournaments.
33. Saturday flea market – in the parking lot as a fund raiser.
34. Plastics clinic and spa
35. Issue I.D. cards that provide a discount for all goods and services offered at the campus.
36. A good national family restaurant franchise such as Carrow's or Denney's.
37. Publish a newsletter – not about you, but about them. Print articles about patients and former patients, their life success and tragedies, births, graduations, businesses, heroes. Your hospital, and your restaurant/stores/clinics/tenants, can get messages out via advertisements in the newsletter.
38. Form strong ties with the community police and fire departments – free use of your education facilities, free coffee, free space in the newsletter, free health screenings. Be sure your paramedic facilities reflect the level of importance these ladies and gentlemen deserve.
39. Form alliances with colleges and universities via providing staff/facilities

for course curriculum that can be offered at your institution.

And much more, but you get the picture.
We all know the arguments – *"We can't afford it, we can't staff it, we don't know the business, we don't have room"*.

We also know the answers – *joint ventures, independent developers, leases to retail owners/franchises, expanded meaningful roles for volunteers, double duty spaces,* - *DESIRE AND WILL.*

The point is, <u>get a vision and drive it</u>. Building lasting relationships do not occur quickly. Unlike a new décor, new uniforms, happy buttons, or new slogans, building relationships is not a feel good quick fix. It is a difficult long-term process having lasting productive results. We urge you to consider these concepts as a long range planning initiative. The risks are minimal. The rewards are enormous for you and, more importantly, your community. **Let's make a difference – together.**

Section Nine

At a recent American College of Healthcare Executives Conference a panel of architects shared with the assembled hospital administrators that "Hospitals and healthcare systems are considered among the worst clients" they work with. Architects are very good at shooting themselves in the foot. Happily I was in the back of the room and slipped out before being identified. I think the panel could have substituted the phrase "most complex" in lieu of the word "worst", but that's just an opinion.

A recent conference for the AIA Academy of Architecture for Health was attended by several hundred healthcare architects seeking instruction from 30 presenters representing hospital user groups – caregivers – on how to make facility design more responsive for hospital needs. Presenters provided valuable information about specific requirements for their respective specialties. There was some limited discussion about interdepartmental cooperation, but much more discussion about "Don't short change me for other departments". Each department views itself as being the most important, deserving of as much floor space as needed to accommodate a highly customized floor plan. A self-contained kingdom. Considerations of shared spaces, collaboration, cross staffing, shared equipment, etc. are topics talked about, as long as there is no compromise to "my department".

123

One presenter asked the architects what hospitals could do to make facility design more meaningful, which precipitated ideas such as better communication, shorter decision processes, easier access to individuals or data, etc.

What was not discussed is the largest unmet need in the hospital design process – decisive informed leadership from the "C deck", hospital speak for administration. In forty-four years I have met only one hospital CEO that would make a quick and intelligent answer to design questions – JoAline Olsen, former CEO of St. Helena Hospital, in Napa Valley, California. She should give seminars.

Although constantly talked about the much sought "integration of clinical processes", or "seamless care path", will never be successfully achieved by the overall design being a patchwork of separate design decisions by independent departments, high admitters, and various pressure groups. These piecemeal decisions are often conflicting and counterproductive to achieving an optimal total design. The result is lots of good ideas without a unifying leadership, a depressing (but true) observation which answers in part why healthcare construction costs and schedules are out of control.

In a building program delays due to indecision will cause costs to rise and schedules to expand. In construction, time really is money.

Another presenter offered the example of a $6M renovation project, custom designed for a high-admitter charismatic physician who moved out of state before construction was completed – not an uncommon story.

Of course the physician's replacement totally redesigned the installation, at great additional design and construction cost plus lost time – more money.

Much design effort is currently being directed at integrating various hospital departments for better operational efficiencies – "optimizing" the care path. To the extent this results in less stress for caregivers and patients it will have a positive impact on healing. From the patient's perspective how, where, what and by whom care is provided is less important than a stress free stay, a short stay, and an excellent outcome. Caregivers pretty much seek the same goals. Issues of operational efficiencies are of more interest to administration.

When an architect seeks leadership from leadership the answer is usually something like "Just keep everybody happy, but don't exceed the budget". Even if this advice were achievable, it in no way addresses the overall goal of better healthcare through clinical integration.

In the design of a department store the individual department managers are (sometimes) interviewed for their vision for a good design. The store leadership then decides what parts of those visions are to be implemented. Input is recognized as suggestions not expectations. It is recognized that the department managers do not own the store, are not obligated for its costs or losses, are not liable for the stores actions, and could well go to work at a competing store before construction is complete.

Why doesn't this process work for hospitals? Because in a department store the leadership knows as much about each department as the department managers, and that case can't be made for hospital leadership.

It cannot be expected that a hospital CEO will be as well trained in oncology as an oncologist and, similarly, the oncologist will not understand the complexities of hospital management and business. However, it should be reasonable to expect the CEO to know enough about the delivery of oncology to make informed and final decisions about the design of an oncology department, putting the overall mission and goals of the hospital first and to have the cahones to say no even to a big admitter.

Hospital department directors lobby hard for spaces and technologies they believe are necessary for best patient care, which they should do. But is their vision for their department compatible with the hospital's overall strategic plan? Has the hospital ever shared the strategic plan with them? The hard lobbying is most often directed to the architect. Shouldn't it be to administration?

It is difficult for architects to understand the political dynamics between physicians and hospitals, thus we are often not in a position to help direct design decisions. A physician may tell the architect "we" are going to install a Cyber knife – typically "we" means the hospital alone is paying for it - not a partnership with the physician. Accordingly shouldn't the architect focus on designing the Cyber knife installation with its "owner" (CEO) instead of the owner's "customer" (doctor) who will use the devise – free, with no obligations?

Well we can't focus design decisions for the Cyber knife on the owner because the owner knows very little about it and therefore must defer all decisions to the doctor. You can guess how those decisions may be fairly egocentric, lacking a "world view" of the hospital's strategic plan.

So how can we bridge the knowledge gap between administration's concerns for strategy, mission, public commitment, long term planning and economics, and the concerns of physician/users of spaces and technologies for safety, quality, good outcomes, efficiency and patient friendly environments?

While expert consultants are available for technology coordination, program administration, or project management there appears to be no single source that combines the total knowledge base that leadership can rely upon.

Perhaps a hospital could assemble an independent advisory board for the project, having expert representations from administrative and clinical backgrounds, which could provide a dispassionate third party evaluation of planning decisions. It is not suggested that the advisory board totally drive a project design, but instead be a knowledgeable resource for decision making and a buffer to help ameliorate contentious views.

There are many consultants who purport to provide such expert advice – program managers, project managers, master planners, strategic planners, etc. Few – if any – have all the decision skills needed in house. Instead they act as brokers who hire special expertise for resale to the hospital.

No decision system will be perfect, especially in the highly complex process of healthcare design. Perhaps the phrase "healthcare design" is a key – defining what specific aspects of healthcare are driving each design decision, by example healthcare design of: facilities, services, reimbursements, staffing, technologies, economics, systems, etc. ad infinitum and the interactions between them. The answer is the problem – all of them drive each other.

How about a rest?

I never tire of watching the surf. It is at the same time peaceful and terrifying, relaxing and stimulating, ever-changing and changeless. Physical contact

BEFORE YOU TRY TO ESCAPE, KNOW WHERE TO.

between alien worlds affords symbolisms from which endless postulates spring. Food not just for the eye but also – more so – for the mind.

To witness a precise and restless boundary between alien existences can command my constant and amazed attention. Although occasional explorers scurry between these worlds – crabs, seals, etc. little dialogue occurs between my world and the surging unknown beyond the surf line, · or shoreline, depending on your point of view.

Laguna, 1980

Section Ten

There will now be a brief intermission while I watch my Joany greet the day, and have our morning coffee. My gal is an evolutionary aberration. Somewhere long ago and far away nature mixed the gene pool of fauna and flora, resulting in people like Joany. To watch her bump around the house until all synapses are finally connected properly is very entertaining. Her wake/sleep modes are tied directly to sunlight. A veritable human sun flower. Accordingly we have our coffee very early in summer, and very late in winter.

This morning's coffee topic is Joany informing me of how many fragmented sentences the computer has detected so far in this book. My recommendation is to switch that function off. Permanently. My whole thought process is fragmented so what does it expect? Well, my morning glory has unfurled, so it's back to work, if you can call this work. Without my morning glory there would be no book. And without her there would be no me.

As they say, no matter how much you push an envelope, it will still be stationery. Another one I like: If you throw a bomb into a French kitchen, it could result in linoleum blown apart.

As I write this a serious debate is raging in Washington over our healthcare system, with some proposals suggesting replacement in lieu of repair. The replacement scenarios, masked as a series of incremental "options", have a government controlled healthcare at the end.

The "crises" that presented the opportunity to toss out healthcare as we know it and replace it with a "Government" option is the presence of uninsured in our midst. The number of millions swarming the streets with no healthcare <u>insurance</u>. That is not to say without healthcare <u>treatment</u>. By law those persons presenting to a hospital that accepts Medicaid must receive treatment. They are just without healthcare insurance. How that 45 million is broken down is interesting, and highly debatable, but even more intriguing is where the number came from – the 2005 U.S. Census Bureau's Current Population Survey (CPS). Another Census Bureau Survey, The Survey of Income and Program Participation (SIPP), estimates about 23 million uninsured. Statistics are the weapon of choice in politics so if a bigger number makes a better case for your crises, use it.

My conservative buddies see darkness in every corner of a government run health system. By example they fear healthcare will be rationed. Of course it will because it already is. "Universal access" will not mean "unlimited access". Currently access to healthcare procedures is "rationed" by a patient's proximity to facilities that provide advanced technologies, insurance restrictions, religious dictates, long waiting lines, scarcity, etc. If there are not enough donor hearts for everyone, the sickest will go to the front of the rationing line.

Or we could use the "progressives" philosophy and throw all the donor hearts away so everyone has an equal chance of dying. Healthcare can not be immune to the laws of supply and demand and when demand outstrips supply – a common occurrence – there will <u>continue</u> to be rationing.

Supposedly part of the proposal is that individuals must have an end of life plan, with counseling being a mandatory part of the healthcare coverage. That is a hot potato! Nobody wants to contemplate their personal demise, and will resist being forced to do so. A bit of dumb marketing. Structuring a personal directive for medical care is a good thing to do – <u>when I</u> decide to do it, and with whom. Other things about government controlled medical care are more troubling to me. I have had the same family doctor for thirty-five years – that doesn't work at the Government run V.A. My doctor helps me select specialists if I need one. The V.A. assigns whoever is up next. I like personal care. I like my doctor to know who my kids are. Government medicine ala the V.A. can't provide that.

In large part controlling healthcare cost will require understanding the blessing and curse of medical science and technology. It is estimated that up to 1.5 <u>trillion</u> dollars are spent each year on new toys. These are expensive toys. For instance a new proton beam therapy installation can cost over $150 million and requires a very highly skilled, highly paid full time staff to run it. How many zaps a day and how much per zap does it take to pay for that baby? Lots more of those cost shifted 10 dollar aspirins.

Aside from the truths or fictions about the quality of care a restructured system will provide, we architects are selfishly concerned about what the result will be on the bricks and sticks – the buildings.

There have been spirited debates around the office about liberal vs. conservative philosophies, and what is a "progressive" ("progressive" is best defined in David Horowitz' book "*Radical Son*", a compelling read) and how hospital ownerships will be impacted if there is a gradual shift from private to public healthcare. Halina Janus, one of my partners and a dear friend, asked me to define Marxism, Communism and Socialism, and how it might affect our clients - prompting this note.

> *October 29, 2008*
> *Halina – here it is – Marxism, Communism and Socialism. As you know by now I write*
> *more logically than I can talk – so I have written this summary.*
>
> ### *Marxism*
> *Karl Marx believed in "struggles between classes" – thought capitalism was evil because workers never got full compensation for their work – the dirty bastard owners kept out money for "profit" – a dirty word. Karl thought all income should be shared equally among workers and owners/bosses. The problem was property and businesses were owned by the owners, not the workers, so the owners made the rules. This pissed Karl off. Then he met Freddie Engles, who had the answer.*

Communism

Freddie and Karl devised the "Communist Manifesto". They believed evil owners – bourgeois – enslaved the folks – proletariat, or workers. They urged the proletariat to revolt against the bourgeois so that the government would own <u>all</u> property, industries and businesses. Everything. In the Communist scenario all people are "equal", but as Orwell noted in "Animal Farm" – "Some are more equal than others". In a Democracy the interest of the people is more important than the government's – government exists to serve its citizens. In Communism the interest of government is more important than individuals or groups of citizens. No human (individual) rights. Citizens exist to service the government. Totalitarian rule recognizes these classes:

- *Peasants – farm workers*
- *Workers – factory workers*
- *Intelligentsia – us (maybe)*

KARL, THE GRAMPA OF SOCIAL ENGINEERING - AKA ECONOMY RULED BY GOALS AND METRICS SUCH AS "WE WILL BE #1 IN AUTO PRODUCTION, ~~THEREFORE~~ WE MUST MANUFACTURE SEVENTY GAZILLION CARS, WHETHER WE NEED THEM OR NOT. IT WORKED SO WELL IN SOVIET RUSSIA. ?

Socialism

Born in England as "collective ownership" (government ownership) of principal services, plus essential production and distribution systems. It is an economic system, not a political system. Sometimes can exist with capitalism such as "Democratic Socialism" – e.g. England. In the USA the T.V.A. is an example of a socialist enterprise within a capitalistic system. Amtrak is also a socialistic enterprise – our rail transport nationalized – taken from private to government ownership and operation.

In Socialized healthcare – our system "Nationalized" – government owns and operates all medical facilities and employs all healthcare workers – doctors, nurses, administration, dietary, etc. – like the V.A. We have never sought work for government clients, federal, state, or local, because of the overlay of mostly redundant or meaningless regulations they apply to an already over-regulated industry. I admire the end product of care, quality and efficiency as demonstrated by the V.A. Hospital System, but dealing with the Government as an owner has been way too big a pain in the gluteus maximums. A Roman architectural term. Well, Halina, if it looks like the Feds take over healthcare ownership we will have to suck it up and learn to jump their hoops.

Under a socialist system not just hospitals will be dominated by Government ownership but also our huge private market of doctor owned buildings such as medical office buildings, clinics and outpatient facilities. The loss of doctors as owners would remove the most pragmatic, and entertaining, segment of our client base.

Section Eleven

While my firm specializes in the design of all types of health care facilities, we are exceedingly specialized in the design of buildings that house physician practices — medical office buildings, MOBs. Those readers who have been involved in developing a medical office building may ask "Why? Wasn't one enough?" Well, no. By doing many of them, we thought we would be able to develop the perfect universal design for medical office buildings. Unfortunately, there have been too many massive and frequent changes in the ingredients of an ideal MOB to ever make the ideal cake.

The exit of doctors as facility owners would remove the most challenging, informed and entertaining clients we have. Our firm has produced over 80 medical office buildings, most owned by a doctor or — most entertaining — a group of doctors. For several of those projects I provided development consulting services, helping doctors to form partnerships, which is like teaching moths to fly in formation. In all cases a doctor will emerge who has more business/entrepreneurial skill than normal, and can interpret those concepts into doctor speak. These doctors are known as "bell cows" because of their ability to lead the herd. They are vital. Without a bell cow the farmer (me) has little chance to get the herd to the Promised Land. Doctors will believe a doctor. They have too often been bamboozled by consultants, vendors, hospitals, etc. who take advantage of their lack of business knowledge — find a medical school with a course in business. So they trust one another. If I ask the bell cow to tell the herd something, the herd will believe it. If I try to tell the herd the same thing they may stampede, generally over me.

These special doctors are the leaders whose commitment of time and energy make projects successful. However, for their dedication and significant time commitments they are usually uncompensated. Some of my early blunders included giving the bell cows a small discount on buy-in fees, or compensate them out of my fee as liaison consultants. Wrong. Doctors cannot tolerate doctors making money from other doctors – except in the practice of medicine. Two of my mentors in medical office development were Lee Hughes, a close friend, now gone, and Jeremy Cohen, a friend also taken too soon. Their deaths profoundly affected me.

Lee and Jeremy were skilled at being able to hold a meeting with 30 doctors (a challenge in itself) to explain various business issues regarding the building development, each issue having two points of view – the owner/landlord, and the tenant. The doctors were both. Lee once solved the problem by giving each doctor two baseball caps, one said "landlord" and one said "tenant", then worked through the pros and cons of the lease agreement by asking them to "put on your landlord hat, or tenant hat" when voicing opinions about specific lease terms. These exercises in schizophrenia are highly entertaining to watch, but to lead one is draining.

Having a design session with doctors can shake your faith in medical science. For a group of bright folks they have some baffling blind spots, such as a limited concept of spatial relationships, and the laws of physics. By example a psychiatrist client who, in his existing 12 x 20 foot group therapy room, had an 11 x 18 foot rug with a special design (don't ask) that he wanted to move to his new office. He became paranoid when he discovered his rent would be tied to square footage, and each square foot would cost him $20 a year. Suddenly he was into shrinkage (no pun intended) and shrank his therapy room to 10 x 16, insisting that "the 11 x 18 foot rug <u>will</u> fit". It didn't. Well, it did sort of. Rather than admit he was wrong (something particularly difficult for physicians) he installed the rug himself, turning it up the walls and chopping notches where the doors occurred.

Another client, Dr. Stuart Friedman, a Pediatrician, demonstrated an almost complete inability to make a design decision. We did so many iterations of floor plans over several weeks of meetings that he literally wallpapered his office with them. He never did make a decision, except to stay in his existing office and not move into the new building. However, while we would have our agonizing design meetings in his office his nurse would pop in and out asking what seemed to me to be life or death questions about a patient's treatment and he would instantly bark out an instruction or dosage with complete and unwavering confidence. A few years later I applied for a commission with a client who asked what I thought to be a most intelligent question – "Please list three of your previous clients who are dissatisfied with your design ability." Doctor Friedman sprang to the top of my list – I had totally failed him. I got the job in part because the client called my "negative references" and Dr. Friedman gave me a glowing recommendation, saying he thought I was the most patient person he ever met. Go figure.

Among design quirks in doctor office design is that size seems to matter. After designing offices in many buildings for doctors of every specialty something occurred to me (yeah, a duh moment) that the surgeon I was working with, Gene Angelchick, M.D., wanted an office of rather large size. I asked him why surgeon's suites were significantly larger than other specialties and his candid answer – "we have bigger egos". Also larger incomes.

There are weird differences between doctor occupied buildings and normal ones. Like parking. The ideal doctor tenants for parking are anesthesiologists who rarely see patients, and psychiatrist who need to space out patient visits to avoid waiting room encounters of the wrong kind. Low patient load equals low parking demand. At the other end of the scale are allergists who apparently can see 200 patients an hour (kidding) and can singlehandedly overload the parking lot.

Changes over the years in tax laws, reimbursements, etc. have significantly changed the design of medical office buildings. The '50s saw medicine practiced by dedicated physicians who provided care they felt appropriate for each patient, and patients selected the best doctors they could afford. It was an age of physician/patient relationships built on respect and trust – a system since shown by lawyers, politicians and insurance salesmen to be totally unworkable. While it lasted, this age of medical Camelot produced MOBs relatively small in size, custom designed for doctors who had every intention of practicing in the same location in the same way for the next thirty years, until they retired.

During the '60s increasingly alarming signals were sent out from Washington that the Feds had decided that Camelot was not good, and the federal government had better step in and "socialize" medicine, a la Great Britain. MOBs suddenly got much larger, each trying to be a medical Noah's Ark, having one species of each doctor specialty. Although these buildings looked like clinics, or multi-specialty practice centers, they were, in fact, attempts by independent physicians within a referring circle to look like a group practice so that if socialized medicine was imposed, the group could promote itself as a pre-existing condition and thus be able to maintain their long standing referral patterns rather than be "assigned" by the Feds. Of course, these MOBs were merely standard medical buildings housing multiple independent privately owned medical practices. The socialized medicine wolf never came, but his threat had forced MOBs to become larger, and doctors quickly saw the benefits for both patient and physician in having multiple and diverse practices grouped together. For some unknown and unfortunate reason, these new MOBs were called medical "Plazas".

During the '70s, doctors became intensely fascinated by the unique tax benefits their ownership of real estate had on their medical practice incomes. All losses, depreciation, interest, etc. of their MOB could be used to offset their practice income. MOBs were no longer primarily intended to make money or even provide office space; they were used to shield practice income from taxation. The bigger the loss, the bigger the shelter, so of course MOBs got even larger. Remember our discussion in Section 2 about Franks and Ernies? Doctors are all Ernies.

Also during the '70s doctors discovered the art of the branch office. The theory seemed to be that if Dr. Dermy put a branch office on every corner in town, Dr. Dermy would become the only dermatologist in town. Unfortunately, the science of cloning could not keep pace. But their multiple offices did get built, each open just one morning a week. Not to worry, remember the main purpose of building the MOB was not to make money, or to house the physician – its primary objectives were the provision of tax shelter and protection of market share. And so not only did the 70s see the MOBs getting bigger but also doing what their owners couldn't do, clone themselves to multiple locations.

The '80s brought cataclysmic change to the MOBs. The IRS, Building Owners and Managers Association (BOMA), and ADA each wrought massive change. Tax law changes eliminated the ability to use real estate losses to shelter practice income.

However doctors discovered other perks of ownership like being able to jack up their rent to make the building's income stream increase – and also its appraised value – so that the building could be refinanced at a higher value with the difference being tax free income – until they sell the building. There is more to the practice of medicine than one can imagine. Non-physician ownership evolved. Real estate professionals saw the long-term benefits of owning the buildings and were able to use the MOB losses against income from other real estate in their portfolio. About that same time, BOMA became aggressive in its method of determining the size of a doctor's office. Instead of just the square footage within a doctor's suite defining the size, BOMA also added a pro rated percentage of all public lobbies, restrooms, corridors, etc. to the doctor's suite which was and is called a "load factor", passing the cost of public spaces to the tenants. Architects were ecstatic. Lobbies and public spaces heretofore squeezed as small a possible because they were non-revenue producing suddenly became rentable space, a "significant design element", a showcase to attract tenants who rarely understood it would be part of their rent. The dawn of Disneyland lobbies had arrived.

Meanwhile another design typhoon – the Americans with Disabilities Act (ADA) – was on the way. Generally referred to inaccurately as the "handicapped code", ADA is neither handicapped, nor a code, but instead a body of civil rights laws some of which impact the design of MOBs. American Hospital Association statistics indicated that the size of a physician's suite increased by 20-25 percent to accommodate ADA requirements. Of course, the load factor space also increased. MOBs got BIGGER.

By now you are beginning to see why doctors started to lose interest in owning or even renting an office – or even continuing to run their practices. And real estate is a very minor problem compared to the avalanche of bad news they receive daily.

The '90s were the decade of reinvention. Reinventing government, economics, safe sex – and MOBs. MOBs have become group practice clinics, outpatient clinics, "Centers of Excellence", specialty clinics, or primary care clinics. Whatever happened to the Plazas?

The end of the century saw a wave of hospital purchase of physician practices. This new breed of MOBs is most often occupied by physician employees only – no independent practices here. Often these physician employees are the former owners of the practices who, in desperation, sold out to an HMO, hospitals, investment corporations, or whoever now owns the medical clinics, the plazas of yesteryear. Hospitals soon discovered that management systems for running a hospital – those great businesses that think a 2% profit is a wow – can ruin a private practice – very quickly. So many physicians have bought back their private practices.

So what will the future bring? It's been said the best way to anticipate the future is to invent it. Well I can't! I'm just an architect. Hillary tried, but she is just a lawyer. The people who could and should are doctors. They are the only ones who can understand and provide the care, so of course it would be silly to let them direct its future.

Currently the Feds are taking another whack at "fixing" healthcare, so we are in good hands. Remember Mark Twain: "Suppose you are an idiot. Now suppose you are in Congress, but then I repeat myself". Some things never change. I now know there is no universally perfect MOB – never will be, never can be. Perfection is a process, not a state. So we will go on perfecting MOBs whatever they may become.

I just hope they still have doctors in them.

Now that I have pissed off my client base I will have more time for writing a second book. At the moment I am writing on the beach in Laguna Beach. Not a tough duty.

148

Section Twelve

The decline of doctor/owner directed construction is unfortunate because they, as owners, take a real personal interest in reducing construction cost, unlike hospital clients who are interested in maintaining a budget. Doctor owners, as direct buyers, have their own cash on the table and signatures on the mortgage, unlike indirect buyers such as a hospital owner where nobody has any personal risk. Accordingly doctors will seriously question costs, while hospitals are content if the project stays within a predetermined (often erroneous) budget.

The high cost of construction, and the low value of the finished product, is sporadically under criticism by building buyers. As long as buyers think they are "getting what they paid for" (meaning it looks ok and it is on budget) the construction industry is happy to continue business as usual. There is no reason for them to change unless buyers force the issue, and no single buyer is capable and/or willing to do so. Reinvention of the construction industry under new names and processes has become a lucrative field for creative consultants, but produced no real progress.

Recently several new project delivery systems have been developed to save time and dollars such as design/build, partnering, Integrated Project Delivery, etc. All have a common goal – how to optimize the current design and construction process. They also have other things in common. They make a lot of money for the consultants that promote them, and they all have a poor record of consistently achieving lower cost and higher value.

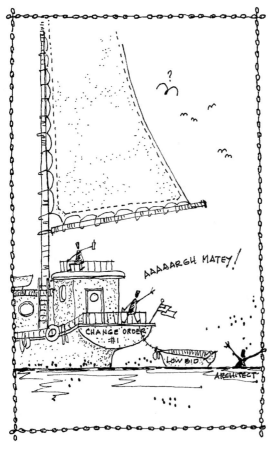

Over the last forty-six years our firm has performed 85% of its work via some form of process that seeks to connect design and construction to gain benefit for our clients. Frankly, nothing has made any significant progress.

Rather than focusing on optimization of current processes we should instead replace them with an entirely new way of conducting the business of creating the built environment. Doing so will necessitate reorganization of the entire chain of design, manufacturing, and installation of building components. Think big!

Current experiments in project delivery share a common organizational premise – some form of business integration of owner, architect and contractor, via a new contract form – an "Integrated Form of Agreement", IFOA that essentially creates a new business entity. Some go deeper and include consultants and subcontractors.

The flaw in the theory of such deep integration is that it forces totally different business to set aside their established missions, core values, business practices, corporate cultures, financial expectations, etc. and magically reassemble into a new temporary company established for a single project. Meanwhile all participants also continue their businesses as usual on other projects with different teams. Anyone that believes this describes efficiency has not consulted their accounting department. Worse yet, as additional projects come to the office they each could require their own newly formed custom organizational structure with new owners and contractors.

Rather than forcing an integration of project participants that requires everyone to customize how they do their work for a single project, it may make more sense to *restructure our entire industry via* **SEPARATION** *rather than INTEGRATION.* "Collaboration" is the current buzz word for the pathway to efficiency. Collaboration does not require integration as a vehicle. Collaboration can also occur in separation. Like collaboration between nations, or divorced couples. It happens.

Construction cost consists of materials and labor which are lumped together into line item estimates, or bids. They are line item bids only if the line item subcontractor is named in the contractors bid, otherwise the "bid" is an estimate, a "place holder" number until the owner signs the contract. After the contract is signed the contractor is in a competition free environment and buys the line items at significant savings, usually accruing to the contractor, not the owner. You begin to see why contractors are not keen to jiggle the status quo.

Through new technologies for preparation of construction drawings is possible to create a complete list of materials for a project at any time. Sweet deal. From these data it is possible to determine the quantities and cost of materials, which could be bid and purchased by the owner instead of a contractor as a separate process much like purchasing owner supplied equipment. Consultants, or brokers, could provide purchasing services to owners who do not have in-house capability, a **Purchasing Coordinator**.

Another type of consultant, a **Workforce Coordinator**, could then concentrate on hiring only the labor component, not subcontractors. The Coordinator's role would be to employ only those workers needed, when needed, in a coordinated management that produces a quality installation within a specified timeframe. In this process the Coordinator would have maximum control over the work schedule because all workers are under its direct employ in lieu of relying on individual independent subcontractors who not only control their own workforce, but also own their materials.

Under the traditional system if a subcontractor does not show up on time, a general contractor does not have much leverage. The subcontractor owns his materials and his labor <u>and his schedule</u>. A Workforce Coordinator would have a significantly stronger control position.

Studies consistently show approximately 50% of time in construction is wasted because of schedule mismanagement of subcontractor trades. That is 50% of the total labor cost wasted. This seems insane until you realize the general contractor doesn't care – he isn't the one paying for it – the owner is – and often the contractor's "fee" is a percentage of the construction cost. How do you spell "conflict"?

The U.S. Dept. of Commerce Bureau of Labor Statistics from 1964 to 2004 show average productivity increases for all industries at 200% <u>except</u> for the construction industry which <u>declined</u> 25% during the same period. You don't want to know the profitability curve. Hmmm.

I have discussed these issues with several general contractors who, needless to say, had a volatile reaction. Curiously many of their arguments actually reinforced the validity of my theory. For instance, I was told several times that my example of an owner's Purchasing Coordinator directly buying drywall materials and the Workforce Coordinator employing the labor to install it would not work because "the drywall subs will not bid only labor because their greatest profit comes from selling drywall materials." They miss the point – we are trying to eliminate markup of material by the subcontractor <u>plus an added markup by the contractor,</u> and we would not hire a subcontractor to provide labor – we would hire labor directly.

My little idea for process also simplifies things like material and labor liens. The owner owns the materials, and controls payment, and a labor lien can come from only one source – the Workforce Coordinator who is directly contracted to the owner. No more potential for liens from multiple subcontractors and suppliers who are not contracted to nor controlled by, and often even unknown to, the owner.

Other traditional practices would be eliminated such as having a general contractor's favorite subcontractor spread his charges and time commitments over several unrelated projects, or analyzing document deficiencies for the best timing to present a change order for maximum benefit. Does this really happen? Duh..

With half the cost of labor being unproductive, plus the significant unrealized savings to the owner for "bidding the budget" after signing the contract, it is obvious a huge portion of construction costs are not contributing to owner value.

So you don't think I'm just picking on contractors I suggest two books more eloquent than I – *"Broken Building, Busted Budgets"* by Barry Lepatner, esq. and *"Contractor's Guide to Change Orders. The Art of Finding, Pricing, and Getting Paid for Contract Changes and the Damages they Cost"* by Andrew M. Civitello

As the role of the Coordinators for labor and materials evolves it is equally important for a <u>Services Coordinator</u> role to emerge that can, on behalf of the owner, hire and direct the myriad of specialized services required to provide a complete and coordinated design. Design professions must also undergo a major change in the chain of events involved in the delivery of the diverse data sets that constitute "the design".

Specialties that in the collective constitute a project's design services would include many in the following list, and large complex projects could well require all of them.

Strategic Planning	Electrical Engineering
Land Use Planning	Structural Engineering
Master Planning	Mechanical Engineering
Visioning	Civil Engineering
Scope Definition	Entitlement Process
Space Programming	Traffic Engineering
Functional Programming	Interior Design

Space Planning	Landscape Architecture
Conceptual Design	Wayfinding Design
Schematic Design	Lighting Consultant
Design Development	Simulation Modeling
Construction Documents	Process Design
Permit Processing	Operational Consulting
Bidding Coordination/	Transition Planner
Analysis	Equipment Planner
Construction Admin.	Equipment Planner
I.T. Consultant	LEED Consultant
Commissioning	Constructability
	Analysis

etc., etc., etc.

Architecture as we used to know it is in there somewhere.

If a system like this that recognizes the value of specific design specialties does not evolve, the architectural profession will slowly be absorbed into the general contractor's labor pool. The role BIM (Building Information Management) will play to expedite this process is explored in Section 17.

Judging from the firestorm this concept has ignited within my own firm, such changes could be more difficult to implement than reconstruction of the general contractor role. Unfortunately for my in-house "master builders", architecture has evolved into very separate areas of technical knowledge and talent. It is rare those talents are embodied in a single individual, and that individual could probably walk to work across the lake. We must eventually realize that these specializations can be – should be – provided by specialists. The point is that in the traditional "I'll do it all" approach there is enormous potential for wasted time plus less than optimal service quality by individuals trying to be all things for all tasks.

Architects must focus on what they do best, and try to remain an independent consultant instead of an employee of a contractor.

Owners also must change. It is inconceivable that an already very busy hospital employee would be given the role of "Owner Representative" for a multi-million dollar complex hospital project as "other duties as assigned", but it happens very often. These poor overworked folks usually have little knowledge of the design and construction process. In the new paradigm (ick! I had to use that word again!) the owner would hire an *in-house, salaried, knowledgeable* person to act as the owner's representative, and to coordinate the work of the workforce, services, and purchasing Coordinators, directing the daily work.

Large national and international hospital systems such as Hospital Corporation of America, HCA, or the Veteran's Administration, VA, have highly skilled and experienced in-house staff for directing design and construction. Unfortunately that is not the case at most hospitals.

Probably there is too much inertia to change business as usual. That is unfortunate because it would result in a highly transparent administration of the design and construction tasks in a process that would allow best efficiencies of time and dollars.

Section Thirteen

IN CASE YOU ARE SUPERSTITIOUS I THOUGHT ABOUT ELIMINATING SECT. 13, LIKE ELEVATORS THAT HAVE NO FLOOR 13 BUTTON, BUT NO... ITS TIME TO GROW UP.

Glad to get that off my chest! Now that I have hospital clients <u>and</u> the contractors fleeing my fan club in droves I am assured of a tranquil retirement, wanted or not.

Several clients have commissioned us to develop concepts for what the hospital of the future will be, with "future" often defined as twenty years from now. Including regulatory battles the design and construction of a major hospital can take up to eight years, so their idea of "future" is fairly short. Nevertheless it is a fun exercise. The result is never what they want to hear, but at least as a consulting futurist you can get paid for telling them the end is near.

In any inquiry into the future of hospitals the first question we must ask is what is the major societal purpose served by hospitals? The generally accepted answer is to provide society with emergency medical services and inpatient acute care for chronic and episodic medical conditions. It is generally assumed that these services are provided for the public good, much like fire and police protection. Of course when you get a bill for services from a hospital, it becomes apparent that hospital services are somehow different from police services. Questions arise. Who owns this place anyhow? Why do they charge for services when the cops aren't looking to make a profit?

In a typical town of several hundred thousand lives ("lives" is hospital speak for "people", apparently in an attempt to screen out dead people who don't need medical services), there will probably be several hospitals, representing several different ownerships – community owned; not for profit; faith based; for profit corporate; physician owned; and various combos.

Although hospitals may have different ownerships, they share many common goals. To provide the "best" care, to provide a "safe environment", to be "patient focused", to "exceed expectations", to have "good outcomes", to have high "patient satisfaction" – (Gee, I never thought my colonoscopy would feel <u>this</u> good!)

They also share other goals. How to steal each other's "market share". How to recruit desirable (A.K.A. big admitter) physicians – especially from rival facilities. How to capture high profit procedures currently done at competing facilities. How to minimize uncompensated care – even the mission driven faith based hospitals. Yes, even the compassionate must make a profit (referred to more discreetly as a "margin") in order to stay in business. Breaking even will not keep the store open for long, thus spawning the dictum "no profits, no missions".

In a business whose charter is supposedly to relieve pain and suffering, why are such competitive forces at work? In part because the competitor control mechanism is in the hands of non-caregivers. The intensity of compassion and commitment to patient care varies significantly from an administrator to an ICU nurse, or an emergency physician to a strategic planner. Competition also exists simply because when there are two or more of anything with different owners, rivalries arise.

So in our typical town, with typical hospitals, way too many assets are wasted in strategic planning, target marketing, positioning and other rivalry based endeavors. Let's assume our typical town has only <u>one</u> hospital, a <u>Mega</u> hospital, supported by a large network of satellite outpatient buildings for urgent care, diagnostics, prognostics, surgery, women's services, clinics, etc. Now how many CEOs are required? Could better equipment be obtained at lower cost than is possible at multiple competing facilities?

Also, without competition our Mega hospital would no doubt have shorter and more productive negotiations with payers who love to play one hospital against another. And wouldn't morbidity and mortality factors look better in the Mega hospital's specialty surgical center doing 3,000 procedures per year vs. 10 hospitals each doing 300? Just like in sports, practice makes perfect.

The concept of a Mega hospital in lieu of several competing hospitals will require an enlightened altruistic age. We will need to put aside the idea that every Tom, Dick and Harry can have their own hospital as a vehicle to make money, or protect religious precepts, or serve favorite constituents. Those are not acceptable reasons for society to give Tom, Dick and Harry a franchise to build their own hospital, and run it their own way. Would it make sense for a religious group, or investors, to have their own police force, or fire department? No. Then why do we permit them to have their own hospital?

Hospitals founded to <u>serve</u> a need, have evolved to <u>competing for</u> the need.

Having served on strategic planning teams at several major hospitals it is clear to me that healthcare is a highly competitive sport. This competitive spirit is so keen that at times it leads to unproductive and even destructive goals. By example, in a recent strategic planning session it was suggested to develop a remote freestanding outpatient surgery and urgent care facility. It was acknowledged the facility would be a marginal business plan that could lose money for several years, but it "would be worth the expenses just to cut our competition off at the knees". A direct quote from the CEO.

It seemed to me a better use of funds would be to mitigate some of the hospital's formidable deficiencies in technology and physician recruitment rather than focusing on the "competition's knees".

It is significant the healing sciences and professions are collectively referred to as the "Healthcare _Industry_". It is an industry, selling a commodity via fee for services, AKA service for a fee, fighting over a U.S. annual market that exceeds two <u>trillion</u> dollars. That can spark a little competition!

Hospitals are like airlines, seeking to operate at full capacity, no empty seats or beds. In every business it is critical to obtain enough market share to profitably operate – no customers, no business. But stealing a competitors market by providing services at a potential loss is a risky gamble at best, and hardly a tactic appropriate for businesses that purport to be a vital community service deserving of special tax breaks, philanthropy, and political support to insure their continuing existence.

At some point we must decide if hospitals should continue to be like auto repair shops – every town needs one, everyone can own one, - or are hospitals so vital to society that commercialism and competition are not appropriate components of their operations? Is a for-profit, (or margin) motive appropriate for our healthcare?

Dismantling our present system in favor of a Mega hospital concept will not occur in our lifetime. It's much like trying to phase out the use of fossil fuels, the economic hardship and the trauma of lost control associated with phasing out the status quo must occur over a long period of time. But isn't it an interesting goal?

Perhaps the warring health reforms currently raging in Washington will come to an armistice that solves these little nagging concerns I have about how medicine is dispensed in the U.S.A. I am told the great learned men and women of Washington are hard after some solutions. But remember Mark Twain's observation: "Suppose you are an idiot. And suppose you are a member of Congress. But then I repeat myself."

But given the stupidities of the status quo healthcare has painted a big target on itself for Congress to shoot at. Supposedly healthcare consumes "too much" of our gross domestic product, but I have not seen a number that would be an acceptable percentage of the GDP. It is obvious that full value is not being received for healthcare services because of waste, fraud, price gouging, redundancy and stupidity. But doesn't the manufacture and sale of an MRI help increase our GDP – even if it is not needed by the hospital that buys it? Dunno. It is way above my pay scale, but that doesn't keep me from an opinion.

Several years ago a long range bomber that was under development experienced one screw-up after another until the entire program was scrapped. The media and anti-whatnots wrung their hands and wept at the two-billion dollar loss. What loss? Over the course of several years two-billion dollars were spent, not "lost", generating jobs and customers for thousands of individuals and companies. It's not like the government held a big wienie roast with a bonfire of dollars. The two-billion was <u>productive</u>, but not completely because it did not produce a useable product – a bomber. But in a way the non-bomber was a success because its unintended consequence was an economic machine benefiting thousands. However, that economic machine would also have existed if the bomber had been a success and gone to production. So assuredly there was a loss – no bomber – but the two-billion dollars spent were not lost.

We can't assume achieving a successful product is the only positive measurement of an endeavor's success. Successful or not the associated economy generated by the actions of an endeavor is always positive for some, negative for some, but never neutral.

A similar dynamic is at work in the healthcare business – industry – profession – service. The repeated efforts of congress to "fix" healthcare assumes the cost of healthcare, at over two-trillion per year, is all bad. But is there some good? Healthcare provides over ten percent of all non-farm jobs. If we cut the cost of healthcare in half, the bulk of those savings will come out of jobs, since healthcare is predominantly selling service, and service is provided by people, so a fifty percent drop in healthcare employees would supposedly be a good thing. Would a fifty percent drop in non-farm employment also be a good thing?

What if a magic pill is discovered that instantly heals all sickness and injury and we could do away with doctors and hospitals and insurance and lawyers (yeah!) and equipment and pharmaceuticals, etc. We could cut seventeen percent out of our GDP overnight. Is that a good thing? Healthcare's seventeen percent of GDP is said to be a bad thing. How about manufacturing at twenty percent of GDP – shouldn't we try to reduce that? Or is manufacturing good, but healthcare bad.

I guess producing toasters and vibrators is good; producing surgeries and vaccines is bad. There is a paradox in this somewhere.

Maybe the "crises" of healthcare is not it's insurance coverage, or it's cost, or it's percentage of the GDP. Maybe it is issues of value and quality. Apparently value does not enter into the GDP equation because if it did healthcare might not score as a "crises".

A $30,000 car (product) and a $30,000 joint replacement (service) is a difficult comparison. The car has a rapidly declining value to a fraction of its original cost. The joint replacement can add many years of productivity by the recipient instead of a life of depending on our social systems.

Not all services create value, like tanning salons. A better GDP target than healthcare would be the compliance industry, the folks employed to enforce the labyrinth of our codes, rules, guidelines, etc. Compliance for the federal tax code alone consumes approximately 7.6 billion hours per year. Equivalent to almost 4 million full time jobs, making tax compliance a larger "industry" – (producing no product, and questionable value) – than healthcare or the auto industries. Currently the U.S. tax code runs about 70,000 pages and we think healthcare needs reform?!

For some reason Congress constantly focuses attention on the problems of healthcare management, maybe to get the focus of attention away from their own dismal record. Curiously hospital administrations suck up to Congress, maybe for various reasons like:

- The Government reimburses hospitals approximately ten percent of cost for treating the uninsured that show-up in Emergency, so hospitals eat ninety percent. Are hospitals in favor of anything that might pay better? Does a chicken have lips?
- Hospitals fear price controls, so the theory is if you play nice with the boa constrictor he will not constrict you.
- Most hospitals are tax exempt and don't want that to change, accepting all kinds of crap to preserve their no tax but big salaries system.
- Playing on the Federal team can enhance their lobby to kill off the evil greedy doctor owned hospitals. Big competitors!
- Other issues equally crucial to patient care

Back to the GDP. I don't know what percentage of non healthcare service sector employment, (i.e. waiters, clerks, FedEx, mechanics, etc.), plays in the GDP but there is no urgent national initiative to cut them back. Apparently they are considered an essential service. What is a nurse? In our discussion about sustainability I advanced the unthinkable notion of cutting back on manufacturing products we *don't really need*. Doing that would reduce the percentage of GDP devoted to manufacturing. We _really do need_ health, and healthcare. Of course, the problem is a jet ski is a product, and getting granny well is not.

Maybe we are entering a new socioeconomic process, morphing from a product focused industrial age to a human focused age. Our metrics will need to change, and the "P" in GDP needs to be looked at. How can you compare the contribution to GDP of a new vaccine vs. a new motorcycle brand? Maybe we should be concerned with GDV – Gross Domestic Value.

It is interesting to think about what would happen if a truly bad system went away, like a cure-all pill that could eliminate the need for the "bad" healthcare system.

Or, how about if something, an air spray, or something injected into the water supply would eliminate dishonesty and violence. Sounds great. Except, at least in the near term, it would cause a monumental worldwide financial crises.
- No battleships, bombers, tanks, etc.
- No military services
- No lock and key industry
- No police, FBI, CIA
- Shorter legal agreements, fewer lawyers.
- No TSA
- No illegal drugs
- No cop chases
- Arms and ammo demand plummets – manufactured for hunters only – or is hunting violence? Probably not. Just killing humans is

violence. Otherwise we would not be able to kill animals to eat.

It would sure change the evening news – no wars, murders, robberies, rapes, kidnappings, embezzlements, fraud, drug busts – and no media infrastructure needed to report such non events. An honest and peaceful society would initially put millions out of work, and make millions of manufacturing companies, vendors, suppliers, sales people etc. obsolete. If the world could survive the good news, it would be a better place.

Just another one of my good inventions, like my fireplaces for submarines, or my refrigerated sauna. I was going to also list the internet, but somebody already stole it.

But seriously folks ..... maybe humans are evolving a new societal relationship. Several brainy people have written about the interesting condition that could occur as our system becomes more efficient at manufacturing stuff and growing food and therefore more "free time" – (there is no such thing by the way) – will be available to members of the tribe. Not everyone will need to work frantically 24/7 like in the good old days, just to make essentials for the tribe like food, shelter, and war. Sounds good so far.

Unfortunately as the work load decreases if nothing is developed to occupy non-working time, sloth will fill in, which can be a good thing. Sloth begat the art of just fooling around with stuff like sticks and rocks which evolved into becoming proficient at neat new things like communication, dance, painting, sculpture, thinking and, of course, better weapons.

Currently there is a worldwide financial crunch resulting in a daily reporting of the constantly increasing percentage of persons unemployed. Some of my favorite restaurants have closed. It is interesting that up until they closed they were in full operation, full menu and full service, even with a greatly reduced staff. So the closures were not because continued operation could not be sustained due to reduced staff. They closed because of reduced customers, aka revenues. An increasing percentage of the customers, being unemployed, could not afford to eat out. So far duh, right?

Here is another mythical "what if" to ponder. What if somehow the customers continued to be able to eat out, job or no job? Then my favorite restaurant would still be in business and, if still running at reduced staff, making a higher profit than ever. Certainly there are businesses that have had to reduce payroll to the point that productivity falls. But there are also a great many businesses that have found they can maintain operations with a reduced staff, and a certain number of jobs will never come back. Could it be we are moving to a society where full employment is not a necessity?

If a restaurant can reduce staff by ten percent and still operate smoothly, maybe our problem is not unemployment, but overstaffing to accommodate an underutilized over-population.

Hypothetically a new class of citizens could be evolving that are not required to work to maintain a supply of food and things for the tribe. What will we do with them? What will they do? In our system work is our means to distribute money. The "Progressives" have the idiot solution – redistribution of wealth. How will it work? Read Horowitz "*Radical Son*".

In a hi-tech society the day is rapidly coming when a very small percentage of the population will be required to keep the shelves stocked. At odds with this scenario is an economic system that requires a constantly increasing consumer base (preferably with money) to buy the stuff we grow and manufacture. It's the food chain. Me hungry. You got food. I give you money for food. You want car. I sell you car for money. Me hungry. You got food, etc. etc. A neat closed loop system that only works via money exchange. We get our money by working, but now there is a group that is not working and we don't need them to work.

So the answer is? I have no idea. I'm just writing out loud, so to speak, since I can't speak to you. Some bright minds will someday soon advance the answer. It wasn't Karl and it sure isn't our current crop of Marxists in Progressive disguise, but somebody will come up with a system that does not rely on charity, subsidies, alms, religions or governments to make it work. Of course my answer, mentioned in the sustainability talk, is to reduce the population to a balance between the number of people and the number of jobs to be done. Too simple.

Don't be alarmed. I do not advocate euthanasia, ethnic cleansing, sterilization etc., to reduce the population. How about attrition by having fewer babies? No, not by abortion, but how about restraint? Couples no longer need to have twenty children hoping a few will survive to take care of them in their old age, the first social security system. Maybe the "fertility rate" discussed earlier will actually provide a reduction in babies. Unfortunately there are still special enlightened groups who, through a direct connection to God, are instructed to multiply like hamsters for the greater "good" of something or other. To paraphrase a wise man's philosophy "can't we all just grow up?"

A scarier scenario is society moving the other direction – instead of multiplying like crazy, to instead embrace systematic euthanasia. Hitler is viewed rightly as a monster because of his self proclaimed "final solution". But Hitler was not an anomaly. The list of persons of power and influence that have advanced hypothetical "population management" systems may surprise and scare you:

<u>Theodore Roosevelt</u>: "Society has no business to permit degenerates to reproduce their kind... I wish very much that the wrong people could be prevented entirely from breeding."

<u>Bertrand Russell</u>: "If a Black Death could be spread throughout the world once in every generation survivors could procreate freely without making the world too full."

<u>Margaret Sanger</u>: "We are paying for and even submitting to the dictates of an ever increasing, unceasingly spawning class of human beings who never should have been born in the first place."

<u>Oliver Wendell Homes, Jr.</u>: "It is better for all the world if instead of waiting to execute degenerates for crime... society can prevent those who are manifestly unfit from continuing their own kind."

Recent examples of ethnic "cleansing" – e.g. Bosnia, Darfur – should tell you of "civilizations" capacity for unspeakable evil.

So what does controlling population – up or down – have to do with architecture? Picture the community where you live with four times as many people, and then instead what the picture looks like with half the existing people gone. Looks like two different towns, right. Towns are architecture, architecture that can react to or direct what the environment will be.

To paraphrase a great lady, "It takes a village to make an architect."

Section Fourteen

John Kuhn, a close friend who (although being German and an engineer inexplicably has a creative and sensitive side), found out I was writing a book and he told me that Ernest Hemingway used to exercise by creating a story in only six words that can command a reader's attention. John's example was a six line piece he said was written by Hemingway:

"For sale: Infant shoes. Never used."

Wow! <u>That</u> powerfully foretells a story. I'm sure Hemingway wrote it because John is not <u>that</u> clever, but he did goad me into trying the exercise – "Active pit bull needs new home."; "Her clothes dropped, one by one,"; "Sorry. He never loved you son."; "Thank you for the beautiful flowers"; "A promise feared more than death"; "Wanted: Female companion for extended travel". It's fun. Try it.

One thing it will do for you is to divide your friends into two lists - those who find it intriguing versus those who give you a blank look. These lists will prove valuable in times of trial.

Bingo night at the Elks Lodge in
Telluride. We were among the
first to arrive – 7:30 on the dot –
being engrained with city punctuality
and fetish for schedule.

We were competitive, anxious for the
games to begin.
Town merchants donated the prizes –
dinners, sweaters, skis, turkeys.
Where was the crowd?
We were very impatient to start.
We were eager to win.

They arrived slowly, with the
comfortable grace of neighbors
stopping in for coffee.
Two fat old ladies.
Families.
Singles.
A group of excited school kids.
They were at ease with each other.
This was an old re-run for them, a new film for us.

They were quick to spot the
strangers in their midst, and
to give us signs of welcome.
When the games finally began an
intense excitement warmed that
drafty upstairs hall
As the numbers were called out the
excitement increased, until a cry
of <u>Bingo</u> released a flood
of happiness.

Regardless of who held the
winning card, it was as if
everyone had won.
They were so genuinely happy for
each other – every Bingo was

a victory for the town.

They had come to enjoy
each other, to live an evening
together, to play together.
We had come to win.
just being with them, we did.

1982, Telluride

Have we discussed travel yet? What a great rhetorical question – you can't answer me, and I'm the only one who should know the answer. Well, yes – I've been very fortunate to have traveled to many exotic foreign lands: New Zealand, Mexico, Chile, Russia, Ukraine, Galapagos, Ecuador, England, France, Norway, Germany, Austria, Italy, Turkey, Croatia, Los Angles, Bahrain, Hong Kong, China, Tibet, Botswana, Switzerland, Norway, Jordan, Zimbabwe, South Africa, Canada, Egypt, Poland, Belgium, Peru, Chile, Slovenia, Bosnia - Herzegovina.

In travel I have learned a great many things, and broadened my "world view", as they say. People really are the same everywhere, but their condition and outlook changes everywhere. Peanut butter and chocolate milk trumps all other food. Tolerance is in short supply. Hope and expectations are not synonymous. Happiness lives everywhere. There are too many of us. No matter what country you go to, dogs seem to understand the language. Some people place more importance on their history than their future. A smile is the same in every language. An open mind is the doorway to communication.

We glanced at him when he entered the lodge. He wore goofy polyester pants, an orange and green ski parka, and a black cavalry hat with gold braid trim. He had a pudgy body and a slight speech impediment which he tried to hide by careful word selection. He was friendly to everyone.

He eagerly wanted to join our group. He was traveling alone. He was desperate for friends .

We laughed at him in private. We called him "The Geek". We were so much more beautiful, our conversation more witty, our lives infinitely more complex, more productive, more vital than his.

We shut him out, fearful he would somehow diminish our fond self perceptions. We insulted ourselves by freezing him out.

Another victory for our insecurities. I don't even know his real name.

1980, Telluride

It is very helpful that English is spoken most everywhere, by someone. When Joany and I took our first trip out of the USA it was a totally unstructured venture with no clear itinerary except to arrive at Heathrow, and depart from Heathrow three weeks later. Our stay in England was linguistically challenging –

Brits can speak without moving their lips, and speak an alien dialect of English.

We made it across the Channel by Hovercraft, and to Amsterdam by bus, where we rented a car intending to go to Rome (did not make it until six years later) and while driving through Germany I discovered why we Yanks are sometimes seen as "the ugly Americans". Probably "stupid Americans" is more accurate. Eschewing the autobahn for more scenic – and safer – local roadways I was impressed how easy it was to navigate by following arrows on what I thought to be "scenic route" signs – until I got lost. I asked a German fellow, who did not speak English, for directions explaining I had been following the scenic route, delineated with tourist signs. He could not understand me until in exasperation I pointed to one of the signs, and he explained – "Ah! Einbahnstrasee! One way street!"

Each year since I have promised myself I would learn a second language before traveling overseas. Each year I fail. As you know, I am still trying to master English.

It always amazes me how many Americans we meet everywhere we go, and not just tourists. Business travelers, religious groups on missions, Americans working aboard, patients seeking medical care, students, sports teams, researchers, CIA agents, musicians, etc.

Americans are to be found everywhere doing just about anything – to anybody. A discussion about religious mission work is worth a book of its own, (not here) but I

179

do offer a thought. Bringing instruction in medicine, education and God (not necessarily in that order) to the needy has provided great assistance where it is most needed. "Most needed" is not confined to underdeveloped countries. American missions also serve in depressed areas such as London, Rome and Paris. Paris! How can the French need outside assistance for volunteer work? According to the 2009 Harris Poll the average French worker gets 38 days of vacation per year. Maybe they could devote a couple of days to serving the less fortunate, except their innate egocentric tendencies probably would get in the way. While France is on vacation large areas of Paris have virtually become foreign countries.

One beef I have with American missionaries is the "ultra do-gooder" that takes the kids and travels overseas to pockets of poverty to build a school, or houses, or clinics in a few weeks of frantic effort and returns to the USA chock a block full of feel good feelings. Could they have provided a greater good building houses for the poor in their own town? And instead of flying to Africa donate the money saved (not to mention the carbon footprint) to the volunteer groups living in Africa? Are the pictures of themselves with smiling grateful poor folks really that important to them? To God? I'm just sayin' – there's much to be done in the backyard before we save the world.

Another curious group of travelers are seeking new hips, knees, faces and other expensive replacements parts. The concept of "medical vacations" to specialty hospitals from Bangalore to Singapore is exploding. These hospitals are generally first class facilities that have excellent equipment, technologies, board certified medical staff and deliver excellent outcomes – at costs 70% less than similar facilities state side. What's not to like? Most health insurers like it. But what happens three years after your knee is replaced and something goes wrong? Who do you go to for follow up care?

These concerns are rapidly being addressed, and a new global healthcare network is being established. Exactly how this tectonic shift will be integrated with the healthcare makeovers currently being proposed in Washington has not, as of this writing, been addressed. As usual our foresight does not extend beyond the hood ornament. Probably influencing the issue is the fact that people in Bangalore and Singapore do not vote for the U.S. Congress or President. Too bad.

I don't suggest exporting U.S. patients to Singapore to obtain care at lower cost is the answer to efficiency in our healthcare system. Instead we need to import the Singapore business model to the U.S. Remember the discussion we had about healthcare being the most regulated industry, second only to nuclear power? Regulation equals cost: cost to create, cost to monitor, cost to comply. If a hospital in Singapore can maintain an excellent record for patient safety, mortality/morbidity statistics, and good outcomes with a nurse to patient ratio that is unacceptable to American standards – how do they do that? Are their nurses smarter or more efficient? More efficient, yes. Why? They can spend more of their time actually nursing patients, and less time as clerks doing mostly C.Y.A. regulatory paperwork or unproductively staffing a position that only serves a need for their labor union.

At the turn of the last century physicians formed a group to compare the efficacy of treatment options by measuring outcomes. The organization grew into a regulatory giant requiring hospitals to conform to its manual of procedures in order to become "accredited",

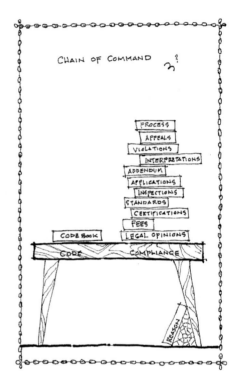

known as the Joint Commission on Accreditation of Hospitals, JCAH. In 1987 they added "Organizations", and became JACH<u>O</u>, concerned with much more than patient outcomes. Today the little 18 page manual of 1910 has grown to hundreds of pages of detailed regulations covering all locations where healthcare is provided, including in the doctor's private practice. The organization is now known simply as the Joint Commission, or to some as "the joint".

As an example of how zealously the Commission guards your safety, during a recent site survey the inspector noted a gurney parked in front of a fire extinguisher cabinet. Checked off a demerit for "inaccessible" fire extinguisher. Gurneys have wheels. Firefighters are not dumb. Hospital staff will need to write a response, detailing remedial action – "move gurney". Wasted time, wasted money.

Multiply this by 100,000 per day and you get a picture of efficiency disaster. There is truth in the adage that time is money. Consider that in California it takes the building permit department the same length of time to check drawings (which they are not responsible for) as it does for the architects and engineers (who are responsible) to design and produce them. Construction inspections are equally tedious. California's construction cost is one of the highest in the country. The process of creating regulations, complying with regulations, and policing compliance is a great job creation process. Like the old jokes says "there are towns too small to support a lawyer, but no matter how small a town is it can support two competing lawyers".

Isaiah Berlin summed up the paradox of the rule of law – "Liberty for the wolves is death for the lambs."

 Section Fifteen

After 75 years of sorting, accumulating, and disposing of my "stuff" a current inventory shows I have retained things that should have hit the road long ago, and unfortunately I tossed out things I now wish I had saved. One thing missing I wish I had kept is a hand-painted sign that belonged to Grampa Devenney that said, "No dogs or Irishman allowed". I wish I still had it to remind myself of how constant are the shifts in the currents of the river of humanity called society. Or, at times (erroneously), civilization.

Grampa kept that sign on his fireplace mantle. It came from the door of a Wilmington, Delaware saloon in the late 1800's and it summarized for me the difficulties of people from a different culture adapting to, and being accepted by, the contemporary mores and customs of our country. Grampa's sign was a summary instruction that immigration, legal or not, causes societal changes, and change means the folks get nervous about who gets what from whom in the changing scene.

Grampa left Ireland as a fourteen year old kid to come to America to avoid starvation. Things were not rosy on the Emerald Isle. The DuPont gunpowder mills along the Brandywine River in Delaware would bring "young lads" over from the sod to work in the company compound for a specific contract time. They were pretty much confined to the compound and were paid in company scrip which could be used at the company store. When their contract was up they were sent back to Ireland where they would be paid off as they left the

ELLIS ISLAND

EARLY DEVENNEYS WERE NOT GOOD
SWIMMERS OR FENCE CLIMBER SO THEY HAD
TO COME IN THE OLD FASHIONED WAY.

ship. Most used the money to buy a return ticket to Ellis Island. The DuPont Mills have been maintained/restored into one of the most fascinating – and unknown – museums of American industrial history you will find. Known as the Hagely Museum, its many buildings stretch along the Brandywine River. A must see.

In the 1800's the Irish were fleeing Ireland for much the same reasons as the Mexicans are fleeing Mexico – trying to make a living for their families, wherever that may take them. If the Irish could have swum the Atlantic as easily as the Mexicans can swim the Rio Grande Ireland would today be an unpopulated wilderness. In the "bad time" the Irish were reduced to eating grass to try to stay alive, their mouths covered with grass stains. That's where the happy phrase "Wearin o' The Green" came from, one of those macabre ditties similar to "Ring around the Rosie's." Look up where that came from! Scary.

Comparing the hotbed of Irish immigrants in Delaware to the Mexican immigrants in Arizona shows a disturbingly different point of view about what immigration is supposed to be about – in my opinion. Assimilation. Wanting to be an American, not just a Mexican or Irishman living in America. Education as an opportunity, not a chore. And maybe learning to speak and do business in the language of the country you say is your new home.

If someone comes into the U.S. just to have a job to make money that they can send "back home", intending to stay here just as long as the work lasts, what do we call that person? Not an immigrant. If they are only a short term laborer maybe the DuPont process is the answer – stay until the work contract expires then be shipped "back home". When they decide that here is home they may become an immigrant seeking citizenship, like tens of millions before them. Just an opinion.

Mexico is a major pipeline for drugs entering the U.S. Mexican drug dealers are often vilified as the reason we have so many drug addicts. Not. That's like blaming bakers for obesity. The problem is addiction which is in the control of addicts, not dealers. If there were no addicts, there would be no dealers. It is sad but many of you readers probably are "casual users", the polite term for addicts. Ninety-five percent of our currency tests positive for cocaine. I wonder how it got there. Every week it seems T.V. news shows tons of coke confiscated from drug busts, and I wonder how many millions of snorts each haul represents. And only a small percentage is captured from the dealer "bad guys". Maybe the real bad guys are the customers.

The "war on drugs" was obviously lost years ago, probably because the war never got focused. It wasn't against drugs, it was, is, against the commerce of drugs. The equation is simple – if there are not buyers then there is no commerce. Harsh penalties for sellers is like attacking a snake from the wrong end. The evil Mexican drug lords are not the problem. Guess who is.

Apparently we have lost the "war on drugs", without a formal surrender ceremony to set a date for our annual celebration of self-indulgence over rationality.

Of course, ingesting danger like drugs, alcohol, junk foods, tobacco, etc. are not the only way we dare Mother Nature to punish us. Purposely putting the entire body at risk of paralysis, disfigurement or – apparently the ultimate high – death is also an addiction for some of us. We have devised fascinating games to tempt personal disaster using guns, bungee cords, motorcycles, cars and other devises in ways their inventors never dreamed of.

Apparently the thrill or high is obtained by nothing (bad) happening. If things go wrong for the "thrill seeker" (aka nitwit) it's a bummer for them and also – and in my opinion more importantly – for the rescue teams, medical personnel, physical therapists, friends and family whose lives are put at risk and hardship so that the adventure seeker could experience their favorite high for one time too often.

My life is not without excitement and peril. Every Wednesday evening an eclectic group of twenty or so friends meet at the Duck and Decanter, a wine bar, to "discuss" religion, philosophy, politics, etc. I am one of three conservatives against a mob of liberals – "progressives" – most of them trial attorneys and retired judges. Fortunately the bar closes at seven pm so the mix of alcohol and vitriol does not reach ignition status, although at times we three conservatives link arms and leave as a group to the parking lot.

Of course the current hot topic is reform of healthcare. My progressive buddies love to point north to Canada as the "solution" to the American Healthcare System. They don't seem to realize that part of America's booming healthcare industry is derived from Canadians coming south looking for shorter lines, and better outcomes. By example recent studies indicate dialysis patients wait an average of 16 days for access in the U.S. vs. 62 days in Canada. If you need the ole pipes rinsed out the extra 46 day wait could be troublesome, eh? Waiting for care has a significant economic impact – on the patient and his or her country because of sick leave (non productive) days, plus untended medical conditions tend to get worse, resulting in longer and more expensive recovery.

In Norway you will wait an average of 160 days to get scheduled for a knee replacement surgery. My fake knee was installed four days after x-rays showed the need. Of course my surgeon had an alimony payment due plus a payment on the Lexus.

Something has become increasingly clear during our "discussions" about the current health reform proposal(s). There is adamant support from the left that reform proposals contain a provision for a government owned insurance option ("public option") that is a compromise position between the true progressive's dreams for complete socialized medicine vs. the mid libs more conservative views. At first I was concerned the "public option" was merely a political moth that would morph to full socialized medicine. My fears were confirmed during the President's speech before Congress on September 9, 2009 when he stated "The public option is only a means to an end" – and "the end" seems pretty clear.

In Federal and State jurisdictions the prison population in 2008 of male prisoners over the age of 55 was 39,000 whites, 20,000 blacks and 11,000 Hispanics per U.S. Justice Dept. Bureau of Justice Statistics. Old criminals are expensive. By example California geriatric prisoners account for 1% of the prison population but consume 33% of the medical costs.

Not to worry! New policies are being implemented to release the sickies to save the prisons money. Of course after release, the ex con is still sick and becomes the responsibility of family (if any) and/or the State/Federal Healthcare system. So what has society saved? Cost shifting is a wonderful solution except eventually somebody gets stuck with the shift.

Section Sixteen

In a project's triumvirate of owner/builder/architect, we architects have historically claimed the high ground, naming ourselves as the project's creators. Of course we ignore the little niggly fact that if it wasn't for the owner, there would not be a project. The owner conceives the metrics and parameters of the project such as identification of a need, a location, a functionality description, a budget, a general design aesthetic (or if in the international style, a general anesthetic), a schedule of events, a vision for growth, a funding source, and last but not least, assumes the risk. Is there a definition of "creator" here? The owner creates these tasks which when successfully executed will be a project. During that process many complexities must be solved – a good many by the architect. That's what we do – identify problems and provide solutions. The owner is the CEO, we are the COO.

The owners create the project via their visions described in parameters and metrics, and then the architects convert those visions to physical reality. So who can lay claim to the title of creator, the owner who created the vision or the architect who converted vision to reality? One can say it's a tie – except the architect's conversions are worthless without the owner's vision. Hey guys, I know it is difficult to give up our egocentric visions of being <u>the</u> pattern givers to society, but how about a little true perspective?

An architect's ego on steroids is called a "city planner", most often manifested as a government employee, or as a consultant to a government. These folks are not the same as land use consultants that design efficient and aesthetic utilizations for independent land owners wishing to develop their own property for specific goals. City planners want to develop your property for their goals to achieve a "public good".

By example the City of Phoenix Planning Department once attempted to "master plan" a large neighborhood of the city that over many years had developed its own plan – which was not acceptable to City Hall. The city planners designed a totally new neighborhood that detailed specific locations for specific uses and asked for real estate developers to submit bids to the city for execution of its master plan. Perks to induce bidders included city "development funds", powers of eminent domain, reinterpretation of existing zoning laws, and "expedited" construction permits.

The "subject" neighborhood had evolved over seventy years containing hundreds of individual homes and businesses, all of whom were deemed to be "substandard", "blighted", and/or in "substantial violation of current codes". Unfortunately the owners of this supposed canker sore on the nose of our fair city were quite happy with current conditions, and in no mood to move. Unfortunately, city planners had a master vision for their area, outlined in criteria of the request for proposal sent to interested developers.

Individual homeowners would be forced via the city's power of condemnation to "sell" their homes for appraised value and take this windfall largess and buy another home elsewhere. Having been designated by the city as substandard housing it is no shock the appraisals were low. So the residents got to go shopping for a comparable substandard home elsewhere. Additionally the developer was required to include new housing (to upgraded code standards) in its plan that would replace all the removed dwellings, and to sell them to low income families. A real money maker.

A similar fate applied to the existing business owners who would be bought out and forced to move to another location – if they could find one that fit their market and budget, let alone survive the loss of business during the migration. It gets better. The city required specific new businesses to be developed in Valhalla, such as a "mid level family restaurant" and "a neighborhood movie theatre". An exhaustive search found no restaurant or movie operators the least bit interested in the location.

When developers pointed out to the city staff that the deal did not appear to be economically feasible, the response was that the city was "seeking developers who would share the city's vision". I asked if the city would share the developer's risk. The project died, but not before consuming huge amounts of city staff time, alarming the neighborhood, and forever tainting the area now referred to as "oh yeah, that blighted area that never got fixed".

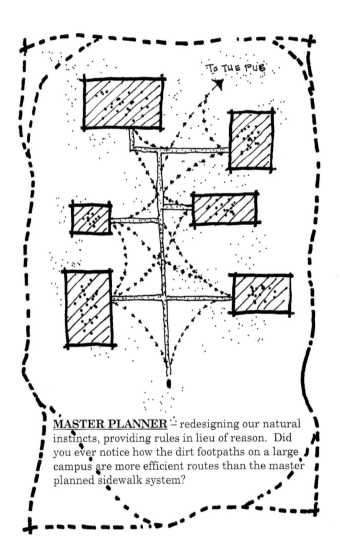

MASTER PLANNER – redesigning our natural instincts, providing rules in lieu of reason. Did you ever notice how the dirt footpaths on a large campus are more efficient routes than the master planned sidewalk system?

City planners do good work keeping the design and installation of utilities and other infrastructure elements ahead of growth curves. Where city planners go awry is when they plan our lifestyle, reprogram our instincts, and try to enforce their own ivory tower concepts of utopia on the rest of us peasants. Planning concepts such as living within a bike ride to work are nice theories that just can't be sustained in reality. Our firm has about one hundred employees. In theory we should seek – <u>and find</u> – a skilled labor pool for our practice within a few miles of our office that likes to ride bikes. Maybe there should be residential zoning restrictions that require a certain percentage of homeowners within three miles from our office to have architectural skills.

In olden times people worked close to their employment because there was no other alternative, then along came an alternative called the automobile and suddenly people did not have to live next to the factory. They could live wherever they pleased and drive to work. Not a very environmentally sustainable concept, but personal choice and convenience seem to trump concerns for future generations and clean air.

The greatest pattern giver to society preached "love your fellow man". Another good theory that as yet hasn't made it in reality. We is what we is. It will stay that way.

Another curiosity in the design profession is <u>regional</u> planners who attempt to provide for the greater good of not just one city, but a whole group of cities. This requires a great amount of vision such as anticipating the interaction of future demographics, economics, politics etc. between the involved cities and the burbs that connect them. This is far from an exact science and explains why infrastructures are usually underdesigned. Sometimes they are overdesigned but we don't know it because it doesn't require disruptive constructions, while underdesign is revealed by inconvenient reconstructions. Often things are underdesigned because of our uncanny ability to breed beyond all reasonable expectations. Sometimes they are underdesigned because of the planner's lack of understanding of entrepreneurial forces. By example if a highway is constructed connecting two towns thirty miles apart the number of lanes designed anticipates the traffic load connecting them. Not clearly understood is that the thirty miles of new road is an entrepreneurial magnet, drawing new developments to be constructed all along it. This results in an overload requiring new lanes, exit/entry points, etc. The road fulfils the old developer adage "if you build it they will come", especially if O.P.M. (other peoples' money) has built a road through your property.

Planners attempt to control human nature via zoning laws, development "overlays", taxation, and political intimidation of various ways, but sooner or later the hamster cage will explode, ruining those beautiful multi-color maps of the regional plan. It is rare to see such plans that contain design options and alternatives that provide for orderly change, anticipating the highly unlikely event that humans will act like humans.

Design has been simplistically, and somewhat inaccurately, described as "Form following Function".

This dictum is easily applied to fundamental artifacts having a static function such as spears, and with greater difficulty to complex dynamic functions such as airplanes, or cities.

The United Nations building, (sorry to keep picking on it but it's so instructive) is a great example of form following a function – a large waterproof box to contain various human activities as efficiently as possible. St. Paul's Cathedral is also an example of form following function, with the added dimensions of substance and emotion. Applied in simple form – no pun intended – form follows function is an inadequate design guide unless function is understood as a moving target. Compounding design difficulty is the often ignored reality that although form follows function, function follows finance, ergo the project budget. Many architects feel their creative juices are impeded by the drying effect of funding. They secretly dream of the day when they will get a client with an unlimited budget and a Freudian complex that makes them believe the architect is their master.

The reason for this recurring dream does not stem from some innate egocentrism but from innate frustration. The art of architecture can rarely be executed by an architect acting alone, without a client. We can't build a studio full of buildings just to try new expressions, like a painter, poet, sculptor, or composer can do. We can't just throw away our mistakes, or keep them in a closet. Our work is a bit more complex. It must comply with a myriad of governmental codes, ordnances, and regulations. It must serve the needs of multiple specific uses. It will require a substantial investment to create.

It requires a dedicated parcel of land – with space for parking. Most of its cost and difficulty is not visible – pipes, wires, ducts, supports – that must be integrated within the art. And oh yes – a budget for the cost of the work – not just the artist's time. Plus a completion schedule that is out of our control.

Other artists can create a piece in days, or months. A building from design to completion can take a couple of years. During those years we cope with daily modification frustration to our work by government officials, labor unions, contractors, suppliers, unexpected soil conditions, weather, and client changes – or worse yet indecisions.

One of the questions owners most frequently ask in interviews is "Can you control the budget?" Cost is only one leg of a project that is a three legged stool – cost, quality, and scope.

Scope plus quality drive cost. Cost plus scope drive quality. Quality plus cost drive scope. This should be a self evident formula, but it seems to be universally misunderstood – or ignored, hoping for a miracle. It should be obvious that quality and scope will drive cost, but apparently it is not all that obvious because owners invariably expect a miracle by telling the architect, who has no control over scope, "This is what I want and this is what it must cost".

How about starting with money, since it is a fixed metric, and say "This is what I can spend – how many of my needs will it cover?" In forty-four years this has never happened to me, so it must be an alien thought to owners.

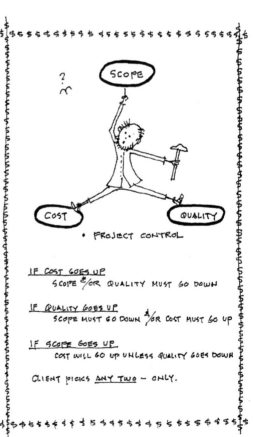

Another favorite interview

question is "How can you control the project"? My answer is give me absolute control over one leg of the stool and you keep two, and the project will be controlled. The owner can dictate cost and quality if I can dictate scope or the owner can dictate scope and cost if I can dictate quality – etc. But a recipe for disaster is for the owner to dictate all three legs. Or worse, make the architect responsible for one leg, but change which leg that is depending on the issues of the moment. In that situation, the architect will not have a leg to stand on.

Aside from budget, schedule, experience and capability another frequent interview question, asked in various ways, tries to ascertain your level of competence in the rapidly changing scene in healthcare facility design, regulations, technologies, etc. – a very important concern. Rather than recommendations from former clients, owners should look at testimonials from governing agencies (difficult to obtain), equipment suppliers, contractors and lawyers.

State of the art. A curious description that increasingly has no relevance. The "state", or current condition, now represents a time interval too short to be of value as an indicator of being the latest and greatest. A stone axe was at one time state of the art technology, and remained so long enough to have significance in the progressions of axe development. Now a state of the art cell phone has dominance in the industry over a few months at best. Probably a more important issue is not the current state of an existing art, but instead the emergence of an entirely new art.

Examples of new arts that had profound effects on architecture in the twentieth century include elevators, automobiles, flush toilets, steel structural members, electric lighting and air-conditioning. Arts now emerging will have even greater impact on architecture. Glass that has structural capabilities and can change from transparent to translucent to opaque on demand. Structural fabrics with insulating properties that allows a building's skin to assume fluid properties. "Smart" structural systems that automatically alter their design properties to resist earthquake or wind forces, and of course, computer software that permits fabrication of any form or shape one can conceive.

Additionally these new tools provide wonderful opportunities to startle the public. Unfortunately some architects, eager to exercise new shapes or materials lose all sense of the need for context or appropriateness in design, by example stuffing shinny metal aliens into a town's rich history and grace. There evidently exists an architectural cult that seeks shock value as a way to notoriety, or instant fame. Architects from Gaudi to Wright have occasionally walked the fine line between sensitivity and shock. By example the Guggenheim design, a bit avant-garde for Wright, but mild in shock value when measured against the highly sensitive and lovingly detailed United Nations building. Mr. Wright once said that a test for whether a building is a good design can be told by if it would make a great ruin. I believe it. The architectural remnants displayed by Ephesus, The Coliseum, and Caracalla Baths give us a clear understanding of the nobility of buildings designed with a purpose and respect for scale, designed for themselves rather than establishing an "architectural statement" for their architect.

Most avant-garde art is uncomfortable to many people outside the inner circle of the artist, being too avant for the bulk of the garde. By example, music that experiments with dissonance and unsynchronized syncopation collects a narrower appreciative audience than familiar compositions.

Painters, sculptures, writers, and musicians can indulge in the avant of their art with their work being endured (experienced) by a select and willing garde and, if not accepted, can be kept in a closet somewhere. Architecture is different. An avant-garde building is thrust upon everyone who makes eye contact and, if judged by the garde to be too avant – too bad. It will remain on display for many lifetimes, unable to be sequestered in a closet marked "failed experiments".

How do these anomalies occur in the first place? Ralph Keyes in his essay *"Invisible Onlookers"* attributes it to what he calls the onlooker effect in the design process, in essence that designers subconsciously design for their peers, not for the client nor the public. They strive to please an audience that is more important to them – themselves and their circle of architectural contemporaries.

Very often we garde folks have difficulty embracing the result of their unsolicited instruction in architectural envelope pushing. Paraphrasing Norman Mailer's assessment "If you are in a building that is more agreeable than the one across the street, the one across the street is probably newer".

Architects evolve in an insular environment, first influenced by their professors and classmates and later by mentors/employers and project team mates. These folks are constantly figuratively and actually looking over the designers shoulder as they work – the onlookers. Assuming one wants to have peer approval in their chosen profession then the likes/dislikes of the onlookers carry more instructive weight than outsiders – like clients.

The ultimate owners/occupants of a project are significantly named "end users" in architect jargon, subconsciously identifying their place in the design process.

Del Drinen's Building – Circa 1965

PHOENIX McLEOD
4433

A lot of this "architectural statement" crap is a result of architects viewing their client's investment as "my building", with pride in the resulting design being more important for the architect than for the client. Fifty years ago a client, Del Drinen, allowed me to design a building for him. As design progressed I was not entirely pleased but Del loved it. After construction was complete we had to wait several weeks for the installation of night lighting for the building.

I heard the lights had been installed, so I drove by about 10:00 PM to have a look. I discovered Del, sitting in a lawn chair across the street, just looking at his building. I parked and went to see if he was ok and he told me he had been sitting there for an hour, just looking. He was very emotional over the fact that he had created his building, his contribution to his community, and was filled with pride. I will admit that on a scale of one to ten for an aesthetic success that I would have liked to achieve, we scored a low five. But I still view that building as one of my most successful and satisfying projects ever, with great pride.

I don't suggest that an architect should merely be a drafting service somehow copying sketches from the owner's mind. For starters there is the problem that the owner could be more than one person, thereby giving schizophrenic directions.

I do suggest an architect should create an aesthetic and function that incorporates the <u>owner's</u> tastes and needs as much as possible while adhering to the basic principles of design, governing restrictions, and respect for adjacent architecture.

These beliefs account for why you are not reading a book about a famous architect, but instead just about me. It is because I always designed for the client's taste that I never developed a "style" of my own. Without a special style you will never be famous.

I was gong to say talent is also an important ingredient, but then I thought about all of the dysfunctional, in your face, out of context, out of budget (a project's first requirement) projects that seem to represent "talent" today and I changed my mind. Maybe talent has more to do with successfully serving the client instead of an architect's need to make a statement with the client's money to further his or her style. I am an architect that values Del Drinen as a successful project in lieu of a slick magazine spread. Fortunately there are a lot of us.

Section Seventeen

Which brings me to the ethics of architecture, or what's left of it. Not the smoothest segue, eh? When I began my practice in the olden days, the American Institute of Architects Chapter that I belonged to had an ethics committee. One of the ethics monitored by the committee involved competition. It was unethical to attempt to steal a fellow architects clients, to publish advertisements, to recruit a competitors staff, to offer free service to obtain work, etc. Sort of a combination of ethics, civility and collaboration to define a profession.

It is the collaboration thing that got us into trouble. In the late 80s the Feds got around to applying the Sherman Antitrust Act to the practice of architecture, meaning among other things we could no longer have a fixed fee structure that everyone adhered to, thus allowing less capable architects to obtain work by cutting their fees and "shopping" for the cheapest engineering consultant.

When asked what he feared most about his job one of our astronauts said "worrying about sitting on top of a highly complex extremely volatile construction containing thousands of critical parts, each one supplied by the lowest bidder."

Say you want a brick wall of a specific brick quality, eight feet high and a hundred feet long with the lowest

209

possible cost the main criteria. Assume what the low bid system will do is find the mason who pays his help less, or accepts less profit, or what? Steals the bricks? Probably he will build it with more attention to speed (less wages) than to structural or aesthetic quality. The rationale for accepting this scenario is that if it is bad work we will make the mason repair or replace – a real money loser for the project that also really kills the schedule. No. Does not happen. Unless the work is highly unacceptable we will accept it with "minor imperfections". That is what makes the low bid system work – <u>the vendors know they can get by with a substandard product</u>, so they need not factor quality into the cost of their work.

Architectural fees are subject to the same conditions. Before the "Restraint of Trade" requirements, architectural fees were set for projects of various size and complexity. It was assumed a baseline fee existed required to produce quality services for special categories of projects. Unfortunately there was another assumption – that all architects are created equal, therefore producing equal quality. Market forces tended to solve this problem by word getting around that Dumsit Architects, Ltd did bad work. Because of fees being fixed, and cutting them breached AIA ethics, the Dumsit firms gradually failed from lack of work. But when fee control was lifted, the Dumsits had a new weapon – lower fees, and a vicious weapon it was. Architects charging fees appropriate to the level of capability and experience required to design a project were seen as price gouging when compared to Dumsit's fees.

So began the era of architectural selection via a "Request for Proposal", basically asking "What will you do and what will you charge". Sometimes the RFP is preceded by an RFQ, a Request for Qualifications. Sometimes the RFP and RFQ are incorporated into a single document. Regardless of how it is packaged – RFQ, RFP, RFQP – it is a thinly veiled bidding war. Expectations are that the services provided will have equal quality among the bidders, so the comparative metrics are speed and cost, enabling a quixotic quest for the highest quality for the lowest cost.

Products can be physically retrospectively compared for quality, but services must be proscriptedly compared for quality, based on research, metric comparisons and assumptions that future service and quality will be equal to past performance. This makes shopping for service very difficult for metric driven managers, so after all the probing questions about quality are looked at the main decider is asked – "What's your fee." Bingo! A metric to compare!

One bizarre selection practice that has hopefully begun to die out is the "design competition". A group of design firms are given a project description and invited to submit a design solution with all submittals juried by a panel of experts who select a winner. In early times invited designers received no compensation but now a "stipend" is often provided, which barely covers paper supplies.

The bulk of an architect's fee and the overwhelming value of their service is for the design solution phase of their work. Ego driven firms are willing to risk the whole banana going for the brass ring. Of course there is no guarantee the project will even go forward after the competition, compounding the risk – a lunacy made possible because architects are very gullible. What would happen if I asked five auto designers to each design a car at no cost to me and then I will choose which one I like best and, perhaps, buy it? Yes – five auto designers would think me insane.

Competitions are best suited for projects having minimum and specific goals, such as the design of memorials, literary or musical compositions, or chili cook-offs. These sorts of competitions do not require the massive commitment of a firm's assets to design a building, or a town center. In fact they are well suited for individuals or groups of students or freelance artists.

A magnificent result of such competition is the Vietnam War Memorial in Washington D.C., one of the most moving architectural experiences you can find. It was designed by a Yale student as a design challenge who received a grade of "B" by her apparently unemotional professor. Fortunately, in spite of her professor's expert assessment, Maya Ying Lin submitted her solution to the national competition and was selected out of over 1,500 entries by a unanimous jury decision. Go Maya!

The computer industry sized up architects early as being business inert. The first systems for computer assisted drafting and design was marketed as a way to greater production speed and therefore, supposedly, less production cost. A double whammy! Now we could offer our services faster than our competitor, and by deducting our reduced cost from our fee, we could be cheaper than the competition. Faster and cheaper, a formidable marketing weapon.

Architects, of course, missed the value of computers – the ability to rapidly investigate multiple design options, detect defects, increase cross discipline communications, and produce higher quality document information for builders, agencies, and suppliers. Any money saved in production could, should, be reinvested in the firm for education, research and technology instead of used to reduce fees. Further evidence of my professions' business acumen is our brilliant idea that we could recoup the cost of a computer system by listing its use as an "additional service" in early versions of the A.I.A. owner/architect contract. It was a tough sell that soon died, and the "additional service" was eliminated from contracts.

Clients don't care how the documents are produced. They figure they are paying to have drawings, and they don't care if the architects use charcoal and parchment, Crayolas, or a fancy new machine. Clients expect quality documents and are not concerned about how they are produced. The AIA soon discovered charging for the means of production would not fly. The client will pay for the documents, but not for how they are produced.

But we persist. Recent computer advances have become increasingly costly to integrate into an architectural firm, by example BIM. The boys and girls of architecture are at it again, charging extra to use it. Clients are resisting paying for it. "Déjà vu all over again" – Yogi Berra. Einstein said it best: "The sign of insanity is doing the same thing over and over expecting a different result".

BIM, Building Information Modeling (Also called Management), is a powerful computer application that allows all project participants to have constant real time interaction and access to all project engineering, design, economic, schedule and other data and documents. General contractors immediately understood that although BIM provides a powerful tool for collaboration only one participant can be central control for data management and they have already gained the high ground. Some think the manager should be the architects, but as usual architects are too fascinated with design opportunities and have missed the business opportunities.

BIM's prehistoric ancestor, D/B, Design Build, forged builder and designer into a "seamless" entity. D/B emerged as a saleable service – supposedly a process to eliminate conflicts between architect and contractor and giving owners a single point of responsibility. Contractors understood immediately that responsibility equaled control.

Accordingly D/B rapidly became a process of contractors hiring the architect, thus the architect's responsibility was to the contractor instead of the owner. This barrier between owner and architect did not sit well with me, exacerbated by a clause contractors insert in the D/B contract between contractor/architect that forbids the architect from having meetings with the owner without a contractor representative being present. Sort of sets the tone of trust, don't you think?

The incompatibility in D/B stems from a difference in goals. Contractors are selling product and their primary goals are "on time and on budget". Architects are selling services and their primary goals are functionality and durability. Rushing design that may result in less than optimal functional solutions does not concern the contractor. If the project opens on schedule and on budget the contractor is a hero. Later, when the owner settles into operation, missed opportunities for functionality are discovered which, of course, are the architect's fault because, as the contractor will tell you, "we only build what the architect draws". I wish they did.

I became unpopular with contractors by performing D/B contracts that were design lead vs. builder lead, where architects hire contractors to work for them. Under this scenario the critical relationship between owner and architect is not filtered through the contractor. I insisted that the contractor participate in all owner/architect meetings.

THRU THE WONDERS OF COMPUTERS BIM CAN PRODUCE ALMOST ANY COOL VIEW OF A BUILDING, LIKE THIS ONE.....

NOT EVERYTHING HAS A PRACTICAL USE.

215

Contractors, of course, dislike this process – loss of control. Contractors tell owners that architects can't be prime because they can't bond the construction risk. Architects don't need to provide a bond – they instead require the contractor to provide the bond. Design lead D/B <u>does</u> work. I have successfully done it, but it has not gained popularity because architects are risk averse, non aggressive, bad business managers, and apparently unaware their role as an architect for a building owner is being replaced as they become subcontractors to the contractor. The opportunities for contractor domination in BIM make the D/B process look like child's play.

Section Eighteen

The following is a note sent to a Phoenix Radio and T.V. personality who hosts a popular talk show. It expresses my views on the cause and remedy of the decline of civility and the rise of violence in society.

April 21, 1999

Mr. Pat McMahon
Dear Pat:
In answer to your question "What can we do about societal violence", I suggest we must take the following minimum steps:

1. Recognizing that entire generations have been taught to <u>question</u> authority, not <u>obey</u> authority, we must develop new social mores which emphasize the <u>value</u> of authority through the use of entertainment, education and news media vehicles.

2. We must accept the concept that some <u>censorship</u> is a necessary component for a free and safe society – i.e. how can one possibly justify free unmonitored access to instructions for bomb assembly?

3. We must recognize that a safe society is only possible in a controlled society, which by definition indicates accepting <u>control of some</u> individual rights – i.e. controlling who may buy armor piercing bullets and for what use.

217

4.	The news media must limit their "public right to know" philosophy in reporting information which, when known to everyone, does not present a <u>threat</u> to the general population or it's governance – i.e., do we all need to know the exact details of every bomb raid in the Middle East? Once we all know our president committed adultery, do we also need to know – have the right to know – every lurid detail of every encounter?

5.	We must accept that <u>duty</u> to societal goals is more important than indulging individual goals – i.e., we now attempt to fight wars with each individual making his or her own decision whether it's the "right thing to do".

6.	We must invest as much on an annual basis in our <u>children</u> as we do on cosmetics or beer.

7.	We must establish for all children a system that will instill a respect for authority, an appreciation of organization and teamwork, and an opportunity to mature. The vehicle for this could be a <u>universal society service requirement</u> similar to the universal military service some countries now utilize, or the LDS's mission system, or Vista volunteers.

8.	We must force hundreds of thousands of disinterested parents to <u>participate</u> in their children's development through mandatory programs via the school system – i.e., parents being required to fill out monthly questionnaires on specific activities of the child, changes in schedules or behavior, etc. with civil law penalties for non-compliance.

9. We must stop deluding ourselves that films, T.V., internet, video games etc. that portray (promote) violence have no effect on society because "they are just fantasy entertainment" – they are also <u>sensitizing society</u> to accept foul language, drug use, violent actions and corrupt government as normal facts of life, things to be expected.

Pat, I don't know how to quantify this last item into words, but I believe our children would be far better served watching real life personalized and sensitive entertainment such as Wallace, Ladmo and Gerald than the canned cartoons and digital games which currently serve as their distraction – without instruction.

Best Regards,

The last paragraph refers to Pat's part in an enormously successful Arizona children's show that was probably as instructive and entertaining for adults as for the kids.

The decline of civility and the rise in societal violence began after the Great War, also known as World War II for the younger audience. WWII was the last war to be fought to a successful military conclusion, made possible because we peasants had been taught growing up that our nation is a good nation that we should respect authority, and that each of us had to fulfill a duty to society even if we disagreed with it. And the war was not broadcast from the battlefield, in prime time color, so we all could see the horrors of war up close and personal during dinner.

It has been said that every crises is an opportunity, especially if the crises is your competitors. Apparently so. Currently the Fed sees our economic depression as an opportunity to, as President Obama promised, "fundamentally change our nation's government". Few understood how deeply fundamental the change he envisioned would be, starting with our national self-image. In every speech our president has delivered abroad he has apologized for "The mistakes we have made in the past". A mea culpa that must be intended to ingratiate himself to the world.

I would like to focus on the good instead of the bad. Our nation, like all others, has made mistakes. Our nation, unlike most others, has cared for others. When America has had a calamity such as earthquakes or hurricanes do you remember French or Chinese cargo planes arriving with help? Are there appeals for donations on Italian T.V. to help the children of our depressed rural areas get proper food, medicine, and education?

Have we made mistakes – yes. Do we need to apologize to the world for them – no. Personally I don't give a grasshopper's gonad what the world thinks of us. We will continue to give them help when they need it and not expect anything in return. I think that makes us a good nation.

About that every crisis is an opportunity thing. The crisis after WWII was seen by Russia as an opportunity to advance communism against capitalism, starting another war, a cold war fought with insurgency, duplicity and subterfuge instead of bombs and bullets. The communist agenda was, and is, advanced in the U.S. by manipulation of our laws and infiltration of our political system. In the years following WWII operatives from Russia, "immigrants", occupied the extreme left calling themselves "progressives" instead of communists, seeking the holy grail of fundamental change – a slow conversion of capitalism to communism without anyone noticing. The phrase "hiding in plain sight" comes to mind.

If you have any doubts at all about this please read the works of Saul Alinsky, especially his *"Rules for Radicals"* and David Horowitz, especially his *"Radical Son"*. And if you can find it a copy of "*The* Nation", May 2, 1966 which contains an article, by R.A. Cloward and F.F. Piven, Columbia University Political Scientist. Apparently those on the left either have not read these works, or they agree with them. The latter is alarming, because the goals and tactics of the progressives openly expressed in their literature accurately describe the metamorphosis of America of the '50s to the fundamental changes currently being rushed into law in Washington. .

If you are not alarmed, we probably would not make good drinking buddies.

Working as academics and activists the progressives have successfully utilized individual rights (as taught by Mr. Alinsky) as a weapon to gain incremental goals, such as abolishing prayer in schools, challenging the

Pledge of Allegiance, etc. The premise seems to be that government must protect individuals from the dangers of majority rule by replacing it with a centralized rule. No more of this Orwell "Some are more equal than others" stuff.

One of the most effective tools in this slow motion revolution was the creation of a single slogan of the '60s – "Question Authority". Of course this advice is only meant to be a temporary ploy because authority will ultimately return on steroids – questioning authority is a dangerous sport in an authoritarian system. The slogan is often morphed by street organizers from "question" to "ignore" to "defy". A few decades of folks believing in this slogan has helped undermine a basic foundation of the rule of law – <u>respect</u> for authority.

Another nifty slogan used at school is "You can be anything you want to be". Unfortunately many kids believed it, listening to stories about how dumb Coach Herring cut Michael Jordan from his high school varsity team, but plucky little Michael worked hard and made it to the NBA. The problem is they can't all be Michael Jordans. Remember Mr. Orwell's thing – some are more equal than others? Now an individual's failure to live their dream is not the individual's fault – it is the fault of the system. The system promised they could be whatever they wanted to be, so failure must be the system – no individual responsibility.

It is true success can come from dedication and hard work. Unfortunately talent is also a key ingredient. I could practice 24/7 for ten years and never hit a layup.

Success also comes from opportunity and knowing how to seize it. In my high school graduation class ('53 old P.U.) one of the nicest and best liked guys was also one of the dullest tools in the shop. I lost track of George until recently. He is now obviously financially successful evidenced by his new Ferrari.

He laughed as we reminisced about old P.U. while I drooled over his car, and he said "You're probably wondering how I ever succeeded." It was obvious the thought had crossed my mind, so he told me his story: "When we graduated I knew I would never make it in college so I took a course in T.V. repair, and later computer repair. I noticed that most computer failures were because of one small part that had overheated, so I tried soldering a little copper fin on one to dissipate the heat. It worked, a buddy helped me patent it, and since then the money just keeps coming."

I was impressed at his ingenuity, and asked him what the part did. His reply: "I didn't know exactly what it did. I just knew that it burned out often". Hooray for serendipity, opportunity and creativity!
Proof that there truly is a kind and generous God.

When George and I were in high school the progressive movement had not advanced to the prominence it now enjoys, so we believed the Army's slogan – "Be all that you can be", not "...anything you want to be". George made the most of it.
I just read where for every eleven dollars we spend on special education needs for "challenged" students we spend one penny on special needs for "gifted" students. Someone should do one of those beloved "metric driven

223

analysis" to determine the "return on investment" of this process. Does it mean we turn out 1,100 "would you like fries with that" workers for every lab technician? Does it mean there are 1,100 "challenged" among us for every bright light? I don't know, but I think a little more investment in our smarter schoolmates would be fair.

School is not the only place where our concern for children is a bit muddy. The legal profession also has a part to play.

About 1935 the Juvenile Court system was established, with the process being that a child would be brought before a judge with no prosecution or defense attorneys present. The judge, with the child's family and the injured parties, would together discuss the child's innocence or guilt, and if guilty, the best punishment and/or education as well as compensation to the aggrieved party.

This process worked well until the mid 60s (yes, that again) when children were given rights, which of course required legal representation to protect their rights. Reason rapidly fled the scene. Recent news reports tell of several states where do gooders seeking to protect the rights of children (specifically boys) are proposing legislation to prevent parents from having their sons circumcised until age 18. I surmise this is an action not popular with Jews, nor will it probably be by boys who at age 18 decide circumcision to be desirable, but wish it had been performed at age one.

The flaw in the Juvenile Court System was the assumption that reason and fairness would prevail. A bad assumption.

In 1964 a fifteen year old boy in Arizona was arrested for making obscene phone calls. He confessed to the crime in Juvenile Court without legal representation and was sentenced to six years in a reform school. The penalty for the same offense for an adult was a fifty dollar fine and a maximum two months jail sentence. Predictably a system that depended on common sense was doomed. Juveniles were awarded rights to protect them from incompetent judges, and unfortunately like all rights, the rights (not necessarily the juvenile) are protected by lawyers. It is not a perfect work.

In the late 60s rights escalated from specific human groups (disabled, ethnic, etc) to being applicable to virtually any single human (privacy, access to a service, etc.) and then, like a forest fire of rights against reason, rights were applied to other animals, insects, plants, and even geological features such as swamps or offshore reeds – "habitats" of creatures who have rights.

A typical example of rights over reason occurred during a wildfire in California in 1993 when about 30 homes could have been saved by creating a fire break by plowing under the dry grasses feeding the fire. Sorry mister home owner – no can do. The grass is the habitat of the Stevens Kangaroo rat which is protected under the Endangered Species Act.. Unfortunately the wildfire played no favorites. It burned the rats including their habitat, and then burned the 30 habitats of the humans who are not on the endangered species list. Yet.

Also the 60s were a time when the focus of rights began to shift from the rights of the public to the rights of the individual. Unfortunately if the rights of each individual trump the public's rights it is called anarchy. A particular fascination of our "social engineers" involved protecting the rights of criminals – or I should say "alleged" criminals. As new laws and interpretations of existing laws picked up steam, law enforcement became more complex. Prior to the 60s the boys in blue, aided by laws to

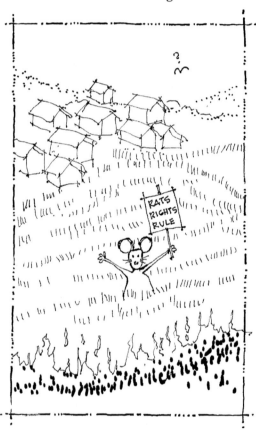

protect the public, were doing something right. Historical statistic show 50% decline in murder rates from the 30s to the 60s. After our social consciousness began protecting criminal rights the murder rate has suddenly doubled in ten years. Of course we can't blame the progressives for all of society's ills. A nation that spends more each year on booze than on Grades 1 – 12 has a grossly distorted sense of priorities. The next time you buy a bottle of your favorite Escape, throw five bucks into a box for a donation to education.

THE END IS NEAR!

CONGRATULATIONS AND THANK
YOU FOR YOUR PATIENCE, ONE MORE
SECTION AND YOU WILL HAVE
LEARNED THE MEANING OF EXISTENCE,

DOIN' THE HOKEY POKEY!

You put your right foot in,
You put your right foot out,
You put your left foot in,
You put your left foot out,
You do the Hokey Pokey and
You shake yourself around,
And that's what it's all about.

WE WERE EASILY AMUSED IN 1950 ...

Section Nineteen

If you try to write a book, keep the T.V. off. I have the sound off, but the visuals have jarred me. A twenty something marine in a wheelchair with no legs. Just thought I'd cheer you up. Something else to ponder – what was worth his legs?

Through the ages it has been proposed that only we old men, who start wars, should fight the wars and stop killing and maiming our children. That could be entertaining news, watching the old codgers whopping away at each other in specialized battle groups like the Wheelchair Wildcats, the Bifocal Bombardiers, and the Viagra Lancers. Seriously, maybe the combat age could be raised to 35, allowing our kids to grow up before grossly altering their lives. Of course, for the rules of war to be "fair" all nations need to agree. Probably that won't work because the animals that use ten year old children wrapped in dynamite as weapons of mass destruction don't seem interested in protecting civilization as we know it.

Not all good ideas are workable.

If pressed into military service my battlefield specialty would be food preparation – for the other side. Culinary mayhem is a high art with me. I can ruin anything. My friend Carol Mook gave me a fail safe pumpkin pie recipe requiring only four ingredients right from their cans so that I could astound the family at Thanksgiving.

I was so proud when I presented it to my stunned guests. It was beautiful, but could gag cockroaches. I couldn't figure out what went wrong until kitchen clean-up when I discovered one of the four ingredients still sitting on the counter – unopened.

The next Thanksgiving Joany forbade me "cooking", but did ask me to put two frozen pumpkin pies in the oven when I woke up (around 6:00AM), a simple request. Nothing to it. I got the pies out of the freezer, set the oven to 450 degrees for something called "preheat", stuck the pies in and shut the door. Being an oven novice I assumed the lever on the door turned the oven on. Twenty minutes later Joany sprang out of bed yelling "something's burning". Indeed. I did not read all the directions, such as <u>after</u> the oven preheats reduce the setting to 350, and failed to read the door handle that says "cleaning cycle".

Did you know that once you start the cleaning cycle it can't be turned off <u>and</u> the door won't open until the cycle ends? You can open the door, but only after throwing the 220V breaker, discovered after considerable panic, smoke, and unkind words like "stupid jerk", etc. Actually the result was quite interesting and could have been a great science project. I discovered frozen pies, when subjected to extreme heat in a confined space, form into crusty black half-dome shapes filled with a sloshing liquid which is quite hot to the touch, and when air is permitted into the oven they generate great volumes of black smoke, which can set off fire alarms and your wife's unpleasant side. Very exciting.

Julia Childs I am not. Don't know why. I am fascinated by T.V. cooking shows and I fancy being able to duplicate the creations I see. Then the pumpkin thing comes to mind. Depressing.

The only successful thing I've ever cooked was a specialty candy. As a student at ASU, I carpooled with my buddy Ralph who would eat everyone's lunch if you left it in the car. Especially sweets. I prepared a special treat – dried goat turds dipped in a melted Hershey bar, cooled to room temperature and packed in a malt ball candy box. I left them half hidden in the car. Ralph ate them. I came to the car and he was eating them. I was sure he had thrown my candy out and put real ones in the box to spoof me, so when he shook a handful out I took a couple and he tossed the rest in his mouth. I put mine in my mouth. _Goat turds_! He hadn't switched. He was eating my concoction and loving them! My only culinary success and I never had the courage to tell him. The ride home was unnerving, listening to him crunch his way through the entire box.

Weird but true. Funny how humor often is about mistakes. I make so many I should be comic of the year. But I am not alone. Consider these (actual) errors entered on patient charts:

- The lab test indicates abnormal lover function
- Exam of genitalia reveals he is circus sized
- Rectal exam revealed a normal size thyroid
- She was examined, x-rated and sent home
- As she fainted her eyes rolled around the room

If you have come this far with me you now understand my not so subtle and not so unique point of the book. Architecture is not just buildings. Life experiences are not solo events. Religion is not only about God. Saving the planet vs. saving ourselves. The future is history on steroids. And my point is?

A discussion about any topic can't be meaningful if the focus remains on the topic – all things impact all things. A discussion about Larry is also a discussion about war which is also a discussion about dogs which is also a discussion about ..... you get the drift.

Probably this little chat should close. I feel like I should ask if it was as good for you as it was for me, but it's probably a good thing that I can't find out. Try writing a book – you will like it. Probably I am like you, read a lot, searching for ideas and reasons. We have covered many topics together.

I hope together we – me writing, you reading – have seen some things in new ways, searching for answers through questions.

Wouldn't it be hilarious if, after all of our frantic searches for meaning are complete, we find that doing the hokey pokey actually is what it's all about?

Keep dancin'!

> _Life_
> _Life is, if not for others, what? If only for self, why? 1956, Phoenix_

ABOUT NICK DEVENNEY

Nick Devenney began practice in 1962 with his friend Miles Stahm as Devenney and Stahm. Later as Devenney Associates, Ltd., DAL. In 1996 he founded a second firm, Devenney Group, Ltd., DGL, to pursue healthcare architecture as a sole focus, plus two support corporations, PDR, Project Development Resources, and PCR, Project Construction Resources, offering real estate development and general contracting services for healthcare projects. Nick has continued the services of Devenney Associates as a consultancy for services such as visioning, strategic planning, peer review and conceptual design.

Nick is a member of the Taliesin Fellowship; the AIA Academy for Health; the Center for Health; The Healthcare Facilities Symposium; the Physician Hospitals of America; the American Society for Healthcare Engineers; the American Hospital Association's Society for Healthcare Planning, Marketing and Development; The Forum for Healthcare Strategists; The Lean Construction Institute; The Design Future Council; and is Board certified by the American College of Healthcare Architects. Additionally, he holds architectural registration in Arizona and California, as well as the National Council of Architectural Registration Boards.

Nick has been the guest speaker for such diverse groups as the National Planning Design and Construction

Conference (PDC), the Healthcare Symposium, Healthcare Design.09, Building Owners and Managers Organization (BOMA), American Nurses Association and the American Society of Healthcare Engineers.

His published articles include: "Caring for Caregivers", "In Appreciation of Lean Processes", "In praise of Staff-Friendly Design", "On Campus MOB – A Medical Building on Steroids", and "Medical Office Buildings".

Nick and his wife Joan live in Phoenix, Arizona. Nick is active in directing DAL studies, as well as participation in DGL management. Joan is active in the Assistance League of Phoenix and is a docent at Barrow Neurological Center. They have traveled extensively and continue to make major overseas trips each year.